On the Waterfront

Mike McCoy

ISBN: 978-1-7366021-5-7 e-book
ISBN: 978-1-7366021-7-1 Amazon Paperback
ISBN: 978-1-7366021-9-5 Ingram Paperback
ISBN: 978-1-7366021-8-8 Hardcover – case laminate
ISBN: 979-8-9875564-0-5 Hardcover with dust jacket

First Edition
Published by Blaster Tech in the United States of America

Blaster Tech
Cerritos, CA. 90703

This is a work of fiction. I made up the whole thing. Names, characters, places, and incidents either are the product of the author's imagination or are used fictionally, and any resemblance to actual persons, living or dead, businesses, companies, and events is entirely coincidental.

Table of Contents

2

On the Waterfront

Mike McCoy

Dedication

I long for the summer days of youth swimming in the lake, paddling a canoe, sailing on the breeze, and running shirtless on the beach.

Making friends, seeking adventure, having fun, making trouble, and creating memories we share forever.

Foreword

When remembering our youth, we easily recite stories of misadventure and harrowing feats but rarely recall the torment of our teenage years; Trying to fit in, learning who we are and where we belong in the world.

When we're young, we don't understand that the pain of our experiences and the struggles we endure are what mold us. We lack perspective, the lens of time, to understand that if we persevere, the dark times will end, and through those struggles, we emerge a fully developed self.

I was thirteen when I faced mortality, death, and questioned the meaning of life. It was the best summer of my life and the darkest days I've ever lived, but that summer made me who I am. Promises kept, and honored requests have propelled me through life and given me purpose.

After all these years, I'm now prepared to share my story.

Chapter One

Mom idled her old blue Chevy Impala in the gravel parking lot just long enough for me to grab my backpack and a well-traveled suitcase borrowed from an aunt. I looked back to see the Impala speeding away in a cloud of dust.

Standing with suitcase in hand, I watched her drive away with my little brother looking out the back window, flipping me off. I'd have to remember to beat him up when I got home.

I wasn't sure why she was in such a hurry. Maybe she was still mad at me. I bet she was glad to be rid of me. I should have been sad, but I wasn't.

The divorce had changed our lives, for the worse. We moved from a modern two-story house in Lake Oswego, an upper middle-class suburb near Portland, to a crappy two-bedroom house in Lebanon, a small Oregon lumber town known for its plywood mills. Mom had followed a man she met in Portland to Lebanon, hoping to snag a new husband. The man's wife was the daughter of a mill owner. That mill produced Lebanite, a hard composite board that made Lebanon famous in the wood products industry. Unfortunately for mom and us, the man had no intention of leaving his rich wife and cushy life. After a short, intense affair, the man dumped mom. With no money to move again, we were stuck in Lebanon.

I don't blame my dad for leaving mom, but he should have known who he married. Maybe I should hate my mom, but I don't. It's just that some people should never get married or have kids.

After the divorce, she was a single mother with two young boys to raise. Mom did little raising. Unless you count the flagpoles of the men, she brought home. She was around and made sure we had food in the house. Other than that, Billy and I had to fend for ourselves. We lived on mac and cheese, and I made burritos from canned chicken and refried beans. I spent my time working odd jobs. Billy watched TV.

We weren't exactly poor, but we never had money. Mom's job didn't pay much, and dad never sent support on time. She yelled a lot. Any little thing could set her off. It didn't help that I was at an age where I gave her grief. She was against most everything I wanted to do. She wouldn't let me go places or spend the night at a friend's house. Mom said we'd have to reciprocate. I knew that meant she didn't want anyone to see what a mess our house was.

The one activity my mother supported was scouting. I don't know if she was hoping I'd get exposed to proper male role models who would make me a better man than my father, or if she just wanted me out of the house. Mom usually wasn't around to drive me to scout meetings, so I had to beg people for rides. I hated that, but she never denied me a camp out or a scout trip.

It was the summer of 1978. The Oregon Trail Council had hired me to work as a staff member at Camp Baker for the summer, a Boy Scout camp near Florence, Oregon. The camp is a couple miles east of the Pacific Ocean and the Oregon Sand Dunes. Camp Baker occupies most of a two-mile long peninsula, a long leg of land that juts into Siltcoos lake like a three-sided island surrounded by water.

I looked forward to that summer. For the first time in my life, I'd be free. Being on staff meant I got to be away from home for eight weeks. Away from my brat of a little brother, away from mom, away from our crappy house and my sad life, just away.

It would be a summer full of adventure. I'd meet people and make new friends. No one on staff knew me. I could leave my shitty life behind. I had a fresh chance at being Danny Novak.

Regardless of what I was escaping, money was my primary motivation. I'd earn one hundred and eighty dollars for the summer, double what I'd earn if I picked strawberries and beans all summer. Enough money to buy new school clothes and save the rest.

At thirteen years old, I was the youngest staff member that summer. The minimum age for camp staff was fifteen, but Mr. Henderson at the trail council office said I impressed him with my strong desire to work. He thought I was mature for my age, so he gave me the job.

Being the youngest didn't bother me. I imagined it would be like the spring break camp I'd attended where nobody knew anybody else. All the boys were in the same awkward situation. You made new friends because there was no other choice. My age wasn't a big deal. I'd been to Camp Baker many times for summer camp, winter camp, and spring break, taking every chance I could to get away from home and earn merit badges. Being at camp wasn't new to me. I'd fit in with the other guys in no time. Easy as pie.

Walking down the gravel road, I studied the jagged gray rocks embedded in dark brown mud. I jumped to the raised center of the road, avoiding potholes filled with water and deep ruts that became muddy puddles every time it rained.

I gazed down at my reflection. Dirty blond hair, hazel eyes, and smooth white skin. People, well mostly old ladies, and aunts, say I'm handsome. I know people say that as a pleasantry. What do you expect the women to say? "Mrs. Novak, what a short, skinny child you have. Are you feeding him enough? Don't worry, he'll grow into those ears." I don't hate the image that's reflected. It's just that you never know what people really think.

I marveled at the cloudless blue sky and basked in the heat of the sun, absorbing its warmth. Growing up in Oregon, you learn to appreciate the sun because nine months of the year you live under gray overcast skies, the days wet with soggy rain.

The road ahead cut a narrow path through a wall of tall Douglas fir trees running from the parking lot, past the caretakers' home, and the trading post, all the way to the dining hall where the gravel thinned, and the road became a wide trail covered with fresh wood chips.

Smaller trails, like veins off an artery, branched from the road leading to campsites on the east side of the peninsula with names like Tyee and Chinook. On the right side of the road sat the enormous dining hall and beyond that, a grass covered field called the assembly area with a flagpole at the edge of the dark forest.

It felt good to be surrounded by nature, where the air was clean and everything was green. I didn't care that my mom sped away. Just the day before, I wasn't sure I'd make it here.

I thought about that night. We'd had a fight. Well, it wasn't a fight, and it wasn't an argument. I guess you'd call it a typical night at the Novak residence.

I was sitting on the couch watching Mayberry R.F.D. on our black-and-white TV. The picture was fuzzy. I'd done my best to adjust the reception, holding the antenna in place with a piece of string tethered to the wall with a thumbtack. Mr. Lee was on my lap; the most recent cat mom had brought home. Mr. Lee was a Siamese, which made him unique among our five other cats. My little brother, Billy, two years younger than me, laid on the other end of the couch talking on the phone, stretching the coiled cord across the room.

Mom let out a shriek in the laundry room. Followed by, "Daniel Lacey Novak, get your ass in here."

Struck with fear, I leaped over the phone cord and bolted across the worn orange shag carpet, to learn what had I done wrong this time. She stood in front of the dryer, holding a wrinkled floral-patterned dress. She flicked her long blond hair out of her face, then lowered her gaze, glaring angrily at me. Her eyelashes were black, thick with mascara and her eyelids painted furious blue.

"What?" I asked.

"You ruined my dress," she shouted, lifting the wilted fabric for me to see.

"Sorry. I thought I was helping. It was in the washer, so I put it in the dryer for you. Can't you iron it?"

"No. It's drip dry. Dammit."

"I needed to wash my clothes so I can pack for camp."

"Camp? You might not make it to camp, mister." She turned away from me and tossed the dress on a bin overflowing with dirty clothes. "Now I need a new dress for… Jim," she said to herself.

"You have lots of dresses."

She turned back at me like a viper, hissing. "If you expect me to drive you to camp, you'd better get your chores done."

"I'll do 'em."

"Do you know how much gas costs these days? You must think money grows on trees."

"I know it doesn't," I mumbled under my breath.

"But you want to go to the movies, you want to go to camp."

"I work."

"Finish your chores then, or you're not going anywhere. You begged me to pay you to do chores, but I have to yell to get anything done. Did you mow the lawn and pick the weeds?"

"Yes."

"Did you clean the garage?"

"I will in a minute."

"In a minute. That's all I hear from you these days."

I turned around and nearly ran over Billy. "I'll do it in a minute. Do it in a minute," he squawked mockingly, looking up at me with his shit brown eyes and pug nose, dark brown hair hung over his eyes. I kneed him in his chubby belly. "Get out of my way, lazy ass."

"Waah. Danny kicked me." Billy cried.

Mom rushed to him, embracing the brat in a motherly hug, like always. "How many times have I told you not to hit your brother?

"I barely touched him."

"Clean the garage," she screamed at me.

"I'm going."

"I have a date tonight. The garage better be spotless when I get home, or you can forget your camp."

I stepped into the piss and shit scented garage slamming the door behind me. Heaps of dog crap and puddles of piss covered the cement floor. Any spot that wasn't piled with junk was covered with crap. That's what happens when you have three dogs living in a garage and don't let

5

them out because it's raining and you're too rattle brained to take care of the dogs, let alone take care of your kids.

The sharp smell stings your nose, but I guess you get used to it. Fact is that smell permeated the house, and our clothes. I hoped mom could find a dress that didn't smell of eau de pew for her date, but I doubted she'd be in her dress for long, anyway.

I grabbed the shit shovel. It had a thick wooden handle with a wide, flat, rusty blade. I aimed for a pile of dog crap mixed with pee. The metal blade scraped across the cement floor. The trick was to scoop hard enough for a clean grab of dog crap, but not so fast that the piss splashed you. It was an acquired skill.

I swung my backpack over one shoulder and ambled along the road to the dining hall. Staff members arrived a week before the summer season began to help get the camp ready and allow the senior staff to train us. I saw a teenage boy sitting at a folding table on the porch of the dining hall. I ran up the steps and stood in front of the table. The older boy stared at me. "I think you're here too early. The boys don't show up till next week."

"I'm Danny Novak. Check your list. I'm on staff," I said, pointing at his roster.

"Huh, I guess so. I didn't know they let kids work in the kitchen. You're in cabin nine." He sorted through papers on the table, then handed me some mimeographed pages. "Here's a map of the camp, and your first week's schedule."

I ran through the grass to the far side of the assembly area, ducked into a dense tunnel of bushes and trees behind the flagpole, then followed a dark trail that led to the west side of the peninsula, far from where campers would stay.

The forests of Camp Baker are old, dark, and damp. Passing through the tunnel of bushes was like entering a dark, ancient land. Dense boughs of tall old-growth trees blocked the sun, shadowing an undergrowth of deep peaty mulch, tangled bushes, Bracken fern, and low-lying Huckleberry covering the forest floor. My legs pushed past fern fronds; their rough swordlike edges looked as if they were left over from the Pleistocene era. Giant roots from stalwart trees with thickly furrowed bark spread over the forest floor and across trails like octopus tentacles, reaching out ready to trip you if you didn't keep your eyes open.

As I walked further, the dark forest floor of bladed fern diminished, transforming into a lustrous bronze carpet of dry pine needles. Walking out of the dark, I felt a sense of wonder as I entered a majestic grove of Sitka Spruce. Saffron beams of sunlight pierced the thin canopy, illuminating the soft golden mat at my feet in a dusky yellow glow.

There was an almost magical feeling as I wandered curiously into an open camp filled with strange cabins sloping slowly to the lake. Music wafted through the trees, the unfamiliar tune, and cheerful rhythm lifted my spirits, compelling a swinging cadence to my step. I felt euphoric. My mood, changed by the new beat told me this was going to be a great place to spend the summer.

I viewed the scattered placement of rustic cabins built on raised foundations that leveled the structures on the sloping terrain. The cabins had a framed wood door with a spring that slammed closed with a loud whack. Wooden walls of the cabins went only halfway up. The high roof and upper walls were open rafters covered with weathered gray canvas, reminding me of wagon trains on the Oregon trail.

Checking my map, I walked to a guy with dark bushy hair and dark stubble on his face sitting on the steps of his cabin smoking a cigarette. He looked old enough to be in college. I asked him where cabin number nine was; he pointed without looking. That's when I noticed several of the cabins were decorated. I was awestruck by the novelty. One cabin had a Hawaiian theme with colorful paper luau girls and a string of paper pineapples draped over the entry. The next cabin had red and green Christmas lights outlining the door, and a small silver glitter Christmas tree mounted on the roof. Outside another, a wheelbarrow sat filled with books and a floor lamp. I watched as a boy carried an armchair up the steps.

In front of the cabins, a solitary picnic table made of thick, gray, weathered wood sat among the trees. Crisscrossed strings of light bulbs hung over the table. The wires, decorated with multicolored swatches of cloth, looked like Himalayan prayer flags.

Walking further into camp, I discovered the source of the music. An Asian boy sat on the steps of his cabin playing a guitar, singing along with a record. I waved, but the boy acted like he didn't see me. I'd never heard Reggae music before that day, but later learned the boy was singing with Bob Marley.

When I opened the door to cabin number nine, my jaw dropped. There were posters of hot chicks and topless Playboy models covering the walls. At the far end of the cabin, there was a large lumpy red ball on the floor, and a popcorn maker on an overturned wooden box. The cabin had bunk beds on both sides with a broad wooden floor between them. I heard hammering and looked up to the rafters. A boy was nailing the last corner of a large black flag adorned with a multicolored peace symbol that canopied the room.

"Welcome to party central, I'm Eric," he said, standing high above on a wooden beam. He gazed down at me with thin, stringy auburn hair hanging over brown eyes and a welcoming smile.

I stood in the doorway with my mouth hanging open.

"Don't worry. There's plenty of room for your stuff. What'd you bring? Did you leave your stuff outside? I'll help you get it."

I lifted my suitcase and shrugged.

"A suitcase? That's it? What've you got in there?"

I stepped forward and the wooden door smacked closed behind me. "Clothes."

Eric's enthusiasm evaporated. He stepped from the wood beam down to the top bunk, then jumped, landing with a heavy thud on the cabin's wood floor.

He sized me up. "You're short."

"I'm five foot one and a half."

Eric suddenly looked angry. "Doesn't matter how tall you are. If you didn't bring anything for the cabin, you can't bunk with me. Git. Find your own place."

His words struck me like a lightning bolt. My eyes stung. I took a deep breath, hitched the strap of my backpack, turned, and pushed the spring-loaded door open to leave.

"Psych." Eric laughed. I stepped out the door. "Stop. I was kidding."

I turned on the step and faced the boy, studying the freckles covering his nose, the freshly popped zit on his chin, and his peach fuzzed cheeks.

Eric smiled. "You can't leave. You're stuck with me. I tried to change cabin mates last year, but senior staff wouldn't let me. We'd practically have to kill each other before they'd let us change."

Eric's words didn't make me feel better.

He extended his arm, pushing the door open. "Take a chill pill, man. Come inside."

Reluctantly, I stepped in.

"How old are you?" I asked.

"Fifteen. I just got my driving permit. I'm saving up to buy a car. My dad said he'd pitch in, but I need to come up with some cash."

Eric let the door slam behind me. "I hope you like what I did with the place."

"Yeah. It's off the hook," I said sheepishly.

"It's all about making the place your own. I saw one guy setting up a stereo system with gigantic speakers, and Dennis, you'll meet him later, brought a black light. Man, this summer's gonna rock."

"Nobody told me we're supposed to bring stuff."

I didn't know what I would have brought even if I had known. I didn't own any topless posters or a flag with a peace symbol. Even if I did, my mom would have thrown a fit if I filled her car with a bunch of crap.

"Our cabin isn't as funky as the other guys, but it's not bad."

I looked up and saw a beautiful model wearing a tiny pink bikini, smiling at me, and my heart lightened.

"Yeah. not bad," I mouthed.

"Hey. You gotta be able to take a joke, man. Nobody's gonna cut you any slack around here. What's your name, anyway?"

"I'm Danny. Danny Novak. I'm from Lebanon. Where do you live?"

"Eugene. I've heard of Lebanon. Never been there."

I laid my backpack and suitcase on the empty bunk.

"What is that?" I asked, pointing to the red lumpy ball on the floor.

Eric stepped to the big round lump and fell backward, landing with a soft whoosh as the ball formed around his body. "Haven't you seen a bean bag chair before?"

"I have now."

Eric stood and fluffed the ball. "You try it."

I moved to the ball, closed my eyes, and fell back, landing with a soft smush. Lying in the chair, I felt a thousand crunchy little foam balls beneath me, making squishy plastic sounds as I moved.

"That is so cool. Where'd you buy all this stuff, anyway? You'd never find a chair like this at G.C. Murphy's Five and Dime."

Eric looked at me like I was an idiot. "The mall, dimwit."

"We don't have an indoor shopping mall that sells bean bags or posters of hot chicks in Lebanon."

"You don't say indoor shopping mall, dipshit. It's just the mall. I go all the time."

"Do you have anything else to set up?" I asked, trying to change the subject.

"I've got an American flag. You can help me mount it on the wall over your bunk."

"OK," I said, climbing to the top bunk.

Eric tossed the flag up to me, then climbed up.

"I hope you're ready to have some fun. Like I said, this summer is gonna rock."

That afternoon, I felt unprepared and late for the event. The other guys were a lot older, and it seemed like they'd been at camp for days, but it was the first afternoon.

Chapter Two

The dining hall, the largest building at Camp Baker, was monumental. Its central location and the fact that every camper ate breakfast, lunch, and dinner in the dining hall brought everyone at Camp Baker together. The building, painted mud brown and trimmed in forest ranger green, looked like it belonged in the forest.

Thick wooden steps stretched across the front of the building that led to a broad porch. The entrance to the grand hall was two sets of double doors, straddling a wide stone chimney built from a jigsaw of mismatched gray rocks held in place with thick mortar.

Late that first afternoon, I stepped into the big, bright dining room with high ceilings supported by varnished log beams. The rich warm smell of bread baking wafted through the large room drawing me toward the kitchen. Summer sunlight shined through large glass windows that lined the walls, giving the room a golden glow. Rows of long tables and wood benches separated by a center aisle filled the room. Behind the far wall was the kitchen, the source of the welcoming aroma.

To enter the kitchen, you passed through a swinging door that was next to a long rectangular opening in the wall framed in stainless steel through which we served meals to hungry scouts' cafeteria style. The swinging door intrigued me. I'd seen them in movies and comedy sketches on TV, but I'd never seen one in real life.

I pushed the door. It swung forward, making a thunk-thunk sound as it passed the door jamb. Its hinges rocked with the change in direction, coiling the springs with tension. The door swung back with less force, almost reaching my hand before it swung back, settling in the doorway. I pushed the door harder, and the door swung wider.

A woman's voice growled from the kitchen, "Care to join us?" Her brusque words startled me. When the door swung to me, I pushed it wide enough to step through before the heavy door swept behind me; thunk-thunk, thunk-thunk. I spotted a large woman with coiffed yellow hair wearing a white apron over a light blue dress. Four other adults wearing white kitchen uniforms flanked her. I walked slowly toward a group of boys, who were all staring at me. Each of them, taller and older than me.

I waved. "Hi. I'm Danny Novak."

The woman looked at me. "You must be the runt of the litter." The boys laughed. "Aren't we expecting one more?" she asked.

"Eric's on the way," I said, scanning the large room filled with stainless-steel tables, an industrial oven, a heavy-looking door to a walk-in cooler, a gas stove, and other kitchen equipment, all surrounded by pale yellow walls that reminded me of margarine.

The large woman put her hands on her hips. "We're gonna feed lots of hungry boys this summer. Just you wait, you'll see," she said as Eric slipped through the swinging door. "You do not want to be on my bad side, isn't that right, Eric Turner?"

"No Mom, sorry. Won't happen again," Eric said, looking at the woman with large puppy dog eyes.

"She's your mom? I asked as Eric shuffled over to me and the other boys.

"No." Eric huffed.

"For those who don't know, I'm Mrs. Garrett. This is my kitchen. The adults standing next to me are the cook staff. Do as we say, and you'll get along just fine." The woman said with a stern look on her doughy face.

A tall skinny blonde guy with pimples covering his face leaned down. "Her bark is worse than the bite. We all call her mom. I'm James." The boy towered over me, standing six foot two inches tall. His arms were long and gangly, and he had a huge Adam's apple poking out of his long neck.

"You can call me mom if you work hard and follow instructions. You might just have some fun if you all work together. Eric and James

12

were here last summer and know how the kitchen works. I'm depending on you two to help train the new boys."

"You got it mom," said Eric.

James nodded and swallowed. The way his Adam's apple moved up and down his neck, I imagined his head was about to fall back like a Pez dispenser. I put my fingers to my throat, swallowed, and felt only a slight bump.

"Jerry didn't come back this summer?" Eric asked mom.

James spoke up before mom could answer. "You mean Jerry the fairy? Does Eric miss his boyfriend?"

Mom folded her arms and gave James a stern look. "We will have none of that in my Kitchen. You boys were so cruel to that sweet boy. It's no wonder he didn't come back."

Mom walked across the kitchen to a set of deep stainless-steel sinks installed below windows on the far wall.

"This week we only feed the camp staff, so it will be light duty while you learn the ropes. Everyone will help with serving and cleaning. James will assign your clean up duties." Mom, then went to the stove and the cook staff returned to preparing the evening meal.

I stood off to the side as the other boys begged James for the simple jobs. "Eric and I will wipe down the dining tables and counters," James announced. I assumed that was the easiest job. Eric pointed at a husky guy with dark brown hair and scruffy sideburns. "What's your name?"

The boy stood stiffly. "I'm Kurt."

"Kurt's in charge of the Beast. That's the dishwashing machine."

James walked to the dishwasher and set a green plastic tray on the stainless counter. "You load the trays with plates, spray them down with the nozzle, then push them into the Beast."

The beast was a stainless-steel box housing the dishwashing apparatus. You lifted a metal bar to raise the steel box, opening the beast, slid in a tray of dirty dishes, pulled the bar down to close it, then pushed a button. The beast groaned and throbbed, spinning high-pressure pipes, spraying the plates with soap and hot water. When the wash cycle ended, you lifted the handle, releasing billowing clouds of hot steam and slid in another tray that pushed the clean tray out the other side, pulled the handle down, and repeat.

Eric stepped toward me. "You're too short for that job."

James then pointed to an attractive boy with thick blond hair that swept over his eyebrows. He had soft white skin, rosy cheeks, and an easy smile. "Who are you?"

"Tony."

"You'll sweep and mop the kitchen floor."

Bruce would unload the dishwasher and stack the plates and bowls. He was tall but so thin and pale he looked ill. Bruce had long black hair cut in a style that looked like he was the lead singer of a rock band, and wore a Black Sabbath t-shirt.

I was the last one selected. Eric looked at James. "What have we got left? There's got to be a job for Danny."

James looked thoughtful for a moment. "I know what we forgot."

"The pot and pan scrubber," Eric and James said in unison.

"It's the best Job," Eric said sarcastically. I could tell by the way he said it, scrubbing grimy pots and pans was absolutely the worst job in the kitchen. I had a sinking feeling that I'd spend my entire summer elbow deep in large metal pots scrubbing off half burned crud.

Mom barked instructions for us to place deep stainless-steel pans loaded with food into the heated serving table on the kitchen side of the rectangular window. We then used large metal spoons to pile food on the camp staff's plates as they slid past. The window wasn't tall enough to see people's faces unless you leaned down, so we filled faceless plates on trays that moved along a Formica shelf on the other side of the window. Once everyone was served, we filled our own plates and walked into the dining hall with our trays.

All the camp staff sat grouped together, filling only four tables in the expansive dining room. Some of them wore scout uniforms, which I thought strange since there were no boys at camp. Eric and I searched for empty seats.

"What do all these guys do?" I asked.

"Half of these guys were here last year. That weird looking guy over there teaches ecology. The blond guy with a mustache is Jack. He runs the archery range. The guy with the beard next to him teaches woodworking," Eric said, nodding to people.

I noticed a group of older teens at a far table wearing white t-shirts with red Camp Baker logos. "Who are those guys?" I asked.

"Waterfront staff. They've got the coolest jobs. They hang out in the sun, swim, and paddle boats all day."

"I'd like to do that."

"Forget about it. You're too small. Those guys would drown you."

As Eric and I walked with our trays, I introduced myself to each table. "Hi, I'm Danny," I said to the first table. "Howdy, I'm Danny Novak," I said to the second table. "Hey, I'm Dan —."

"Are you a ditz?" Eric said, interrupting me.

"I'm being friendly."

"Well, stop it. People will think you're a retard."

Eric saw someone he knew and quickly sat down. He looked at me and shrugged his shoulders. "Sorry last seat, nimrod."

I walked to the next table. It was the table of waterfront guys. I stood at the end. "Hey guys, I'm Danny. You have room for one more?" A chubby guy scooted to fill a gap on the bench.

"I didn't think the kids showed up till next week," one guy said.

"This table is for big boys," said another.

Adult staff sat at the last table. I didn't want to be the pitiful, dorky kid who sits with the adults. That would be worse than sitting alone.

I turned, walked back across the tiled floor holding my tray, and kicked the swinging door open. I stood at the heated serving table and ate alone, watching the others through the rectangular window as they ate, talked, and laughed.

While I was peering through the window, Mom walked up behind me and rubbed her hand on my back. "You're Danny, right?"

I nodded. Her hand felt warm, soft, and comforting.

"Don't you worry, hon. Boys are mean to each other. It's part of growing up. In a few days, you'll be running with the pack."

"You think so?"

"I know so. You'll see."

After dinner was over and the kitchen cleaned, Eric and I walked back to our cabin.

Eric looked at me quizzically. "Why did you introduce yourself to everybody?"

"I was being friendly. If you want to make friends, it pays to be friendly."

"No, it doesn't. It makes you look desperate. Nobody should try that hard to make friends."

I stared, studying Eric for a moment. "Were you and Jerry friends? Is that why you asked about him?"

"We shared a cabin. Last year I got a fag. This year I get a putz. Cabin mates suck."

That first day wasn't what I'd expected. Being on staff wasn't like spring break camp. Lots of the guys already knew each other. They already had friends, and I didn't know anybody. Eric thought I was a dimwit or a dipshit who didn't know anything. Camp was supposed to be my chance for a new start, to fit in, and have fun, but I felt more out of place than ever. At that moment, I ached to be back home.

Chapter Three

My wind-up alarm clock went off at six-thirty. I crawled out of bed, feeling the morning chill on my skin. Eric groaned and tossed his covers off. We dressed in silence, then walked up the trail to the dining hall. The air was cool and moist. The sun rose behind the trees, sending slivers of sunbeams to burn away the morning mist. We walked across the assembly area through tall grass heavy with dew that licked at my boots and pant legs. I wanted to talk with Eric, but he was still half asleep, not in the mood for conversation.

"Coffee. Give me coffee," were the first words Eric spoke as we entered the kitchen. He went directly to the five-gallon stainless steel coffee urn, grabbed a white ceramic cup, and filled it to the brim. Clutching the cup with both hands like an object of affection, he brought the cup to his lips and drank the dark elixir.

"You don't use cream or sugar?" I asked.

"Real coffee drinkers drink it black. How can you appreciate the coffee's flavor if you muck it up with all that junk?"

The only times I'd drank coffee was after church, or at some special function, and I always poured in lots of cream and extra sugar. It was like drinking candy. I picked up a cup, pulled the black handle of the spigot and filled it with the steaming black liquid heated to 200 degrees.

"Be a man, drink it black," Eric said with a daring stare.

I didn't want to be a pussy. I nodded anxiously. As I brought the cup to my lips, James pushed me. "Make way, chump. We all want coffee."

Boiling hot coffee spilled over my hand. It hurt like hell, but I held the cup tight, allowing my fingers to absorb the burn.

James grabbed the glass sugar dispenser and began mixing his potion. "I don't care what Eric says. I can't drink coffee without milk and sugar."

I gave James a defiant look, then took a sip, smelling the rich dark aroma, and sipped again. As the coffee cooled, I drank the whole cup and during breakfast I drank another. I've always drank my coffee black since that morning.

Breakfast cleanup was worse than dinner the night before. There were pots and pans caked with dried scrambled eggs and pancake batter piled around me. I didn't complain. I was worried, though. My arm was already sore from scrubbing. If this week was light duty, how bad would it get with a dining hall full of scouts?

When I'd nearly finished, the other guys were still messing around. James held a white terry cloth towel by one corner and swirled it into a tight long tail. He grabbed the bottom, now holding two ends of the taut wet towel. He then flicked it at Eric's butt, making a loud crack. Eric howled, then spun around, whipping his towel into a weapon. "You're asking for an early death," Eric said, taking a dueling stance threatening to flick it at James.

James skillfully flicked his towel twice, making loud snaps. "You'll never survive my vicious attack."

Tony leaned on his mop, watching the fight. Bruce hurriedly placed a stack of plates that looked like they weighed more than he did on a shelf, then moved close, excited to see the match. Kurt, standing by the dishwasher as always, grabbed the spray nozzle he used to rinse plates and sent a spray of water streaming at the dueling boys. James and Eric jumped back to avoid the spray, then went back to their dueling. Most of the water landed on the floor.

Tony turned to Kurt with a scowl. "Hey, I just mopped that, you pompous ass."

Kurt, embarrassed, dropped the sprayer and pushed a load of dishes into the beast.

Eric snapped his towel, hitting James's arm. "Ouch."

"Get him," Bruce shouted. James lunged at Eric with two quick snaps, but Eric parried, spinning his towel in the air like a propeller to block the attack. Eric swirled his towel tight, then snapped James twice again as he retreated.

Tony laughed. "James got creamed."

I wiped my wet hands on my apron and stood defiantly. "If you guys keep screwing around, we'll be here all day."

The boys met my comment with derision. I'd spoiled the fun. "The runt sounds mad," said Bruce.

"Look who thinks he can boss us around," James said, flicking his towel at me.

I took a step back. "I just don't want to be here all morning."

Eric dragged his towel across the stainless-steel table. "Danny's right. We're here to work, not play," he said with a smirk, then added without enthusiasm, "Everybody back to work."

There was some grumbling, but Tony started mopping. Kurt opened the beast and pushed another tray inside. Even James rinsed his towel and started wiping down the warming table. I went back to work on the pot I was scrubbing.

When I was scrubbing my last pot, James walked up and dropped a pancake batter-encrusted frying pan in my sink. "Missed one," he said.

A minute later, Eric set a metal bowl coated with baked-on batter on the counter, then pushed it into the sink. "Found that in the oven."

Then Kurt, Tony, and Bruce all dropped pots and skillets with baked-on crud into my sink. Some of the cookware I knew I'd already cleaned and put away. I dipped my head, looking at the scummy pots they'd dropped in the sink for me to clean. My face flamed with anger and the pain of humiliation. I knew what they were doing, but said nothing. I tried to push my hurt feelings away as the memories swept over me. This was not the first time I'd been bullied.

It was a rainy October morning when I walked warily through the hallway toward my school locker. I'd cut the top handle off my backpack and cinched both straps tight on my shoulders to make it harder for anyone to steal my backpack. Viewing the crowded hallway, I imagined I could magically make the students disappear so I could walk through an empty hallway without suffering abuse, but no matter how hard I tried, I couldn't make the other kids disappear.

My panic heightened when I spotted Dean Chapman, one of the popular kids, standing by the lockers talking with his buddies. Dean was tall, good at sports, handsome, and had it out for me. He was hanging out with Lonny Manning, Scott Reeves, and Fred Price, the biggest, strongest guys from the eighth-grade football team's offensive line. I'll never forget their names. They all wore Levis 501 jeans with a white cotton web athletic belt, white t-shirts, and black converse tennis shoes. Lebanon kids hadn't moved on from the greaser look. The only thing missing was the Pomade in their hair.

I hoped I could sneak past without them noticing me. No such luck. "Why do I smell shit? Oh, it's pigpen." Dean had given me the nickname from one of the Peanut's cartoon characters.

"What's in your pack today, Pigpen, shit sandwiches?" Dean said, grabbing my backpack with both hands. I held the straps with all my might, but Lonny, the zit faced blond fullback, yanked one strap off my shoulder. Dean pulled harder and stripped the backpack off. Holding it by one strap, he tossed it down the hall. Dean's buddies laughed and praised him.

Dean and his gang had harassed me every morning since the beginning of the school year. I usually fought back kicking, screaming, sometimes crying. They were taller and stronger. It was an impossible battle I would never win. They laughed at my protests. Teasing me was good sport.

That morning, as my pack slid down the hallway, I didn't fight, protest, or cry. I stood defiantly silent. Dean slammed me against the locker. His pack of wolves, Scott, Lonny, and Fred, pressed in, surrounding me, looking savage.

"He really does smell," said Scott, a husky brown-haired boy, the son of a lumberjack.

"Why do you smell like shit, Pigpen?" Dean asked.

I looked up, staring Dean in the eyes. "Because I fucked the shit out of your mom." In retrospect, that was not the best response, but I was tired of being picked on.

Dean's sharp blow to my stomach took the wind out of me. I collapsed, gasping for air as the wolves circled like a frenzied pack of dogs. I jerked my head, looking at each one of them with fire in my eyes, struggling to stand. "She said it was better than getting fucked by your baby dick."

Dean lunged at me, but Scott and Lonny held him back. "You'll get kicked off the team," Scott warned. "He's not worth it," said Lonny.

I smiled weakly. One swift punch to the gut was a small price for standing up to the pack.

Lonny and Scott, holding Dean back, created an opening. Fred Price moved in, filling the gap. All I remember are his beady eyes and deadpan stare as he stepped forward, then, without hesitation, he pummeled my head and torso with rapid punches. I swung at him, but his reach was longer than mine. I hit nothing. His iron fists beat my head like a boxer punching a speed bag. The boy didn't tire easily. He pounded me until his knuckles turned red. My body, involuntarily convulsing, slid to the floor. The bell rang, signaling the start of class. Dean and his pack ran, leaving me propped up against the lockers.

I knew Fred. He lived on the next block, but we weren't friends. I remember riding my bike past his house one day. He and his dad, a big burly man with black hair and a bushy black beard, had gone deer hunting. Their Ford pickup with a gun-rack in the cab's back window was parked on the gravel driveway and a dead doe hung in the garage. I stopped to watch Fred and his dad work on the deer. I don't know what Fred did wrong, but his dad yelled and punched Fred in the face, sending him reeling. He was wiping blood from his nose when he noticed me watching. Fred's expression morphed from hurt to embarrassed, then fierce in seconds as he glared at me holding his deer skinning knife in a threatening pose.

I sat on the floor alone, crying, my body convulsing uncontrollably.

Later that morning, Fred and I sat next to each other in the principal's office. When asked why he had beaten the crap out of me, Fred replied, "I didn't like the way he looked at me."

I got detention for a week. I don't remember what happened to Fred.

James called out to me. "We're done. Why are you so slow? I thought you wanted to get out of here."

I turned to see the guys standing by the swinging door, ready to leave. "Not sure where all those dirty pots came from," said Eric.

James pushed the swinging door open. "We're taking off."

I smiled and waved. "Thanks for finding those dirty pots and pans. I wouldn't want to get on mom's bad side. See ya later."

The guys were stunned. This was not the response they expected. I had ruined their game. But I had learned that if I threw a fit, I'd only make it more fun for them. Getting mad would encourage them to tease me again. The guys had hurt my feelings, but I would not show it. I would not play that game.

The boys, looking dejected, turned and walked through the swinging door.

"See ya," Tony said, hanging his head low as he left.

Standing alone at my sink, I felt like crying, but I wouldn't allow the tears because that would mean they'd won. Why does everyone hate me? What's wrong with me?

I hated my life. I blamed my parents. My family was nothing like the perfect loving families I saw on TV or what Sunday school told me God promised for his children. My life was a bad dream.

I lived in a real American family where mom struggled with her own demons, unable to care for her children because she couldn't take care of herself, and there was no father. He was gone.

It was worse after they divorced. In those days, divorce wasn't common. There was still a stigma of shame on the divorced couple and that shame stained the children. With no dad around and mom in a tailspin, I quickly learned that I was on my own. Deal with it or die. Endure the pain and carry on or give up. End my life.

That's what I thought about as I scrubbed burned pancake batter off frying pans and stew pots alone in the kitchen that morning. At a young age, I had thought of killing myself more than once. I wondered if anyone at school would notice I was gone. Would anyone at camp miss me? Would my mom cry?

But it wasn't the thought that someone might miss me that held me. It was anxiety about what tomorrow might bring, the hope that things might get better, the idea that I'd miss something good kept me going. Give it one more day. Let's see what happens. What exciting moment would I miss if I were dead? Might there be the promise of a better day, a new friend? And thus, I dropped the proverbial knife, removed my neck from the noose of death and forged on, never speaking a word of those fanciful thoughts to another living soul.

Who would I tell? How could I find the words to explain that the pain of life made me feel like dying? I lived silently with those thoughts swirling through my head. How fucked up is that?

I decided if people don't like the real me, I would rise above, become someone else, create a better me to hide my fears and insecurities. I'd smile, be nice, and act confident. A smile was my shield and wit, my sword.

The best way to destroy your enemies is to befriend them.

Wearing this mask, I could move through the world a confident player in the game of life, yet behind the mask, I knew I was a lowly worm praying no one finds me out. If I allow no one to pierce this shield. Maybe, someone will like me.

Chapter Four

During the rest of that first week, the staff prepared Camp Baker for the onslaught of scouts that would soon arrive. At the waterfront, a truck and boat worked to pull the docks off the shore. A dump truck drove down the old fire road that traces the eastern shore of the peninsula to deliver sand from the local sand dunes, spreading the soft golden powder over the hardened mud of the shoreline. A pickup towing a trailer hauled in rowboats, canoes, and sailboats. Staff members stocked classrooms with supplies and the archery range received new bales of hay.

Every afternoon after lunch cleanup, senior staff assigned our kitchen crew to work in different parts of camp. During that week, we helped stock the trading post, setup wooden climbing towers and rope bridges in the pioneering area and cut lengths of rope for knot tying in the scout craft area.

Whenever I had free time, I went exploring. Keeping off the main trail, I stuck to narrow tracks walking through the dense forest where gray moss hung like long beards from old branches and massive roots extended from the base of giant trees reaching out like welcoming arms.

Alone, tiptoeing through the forest, I observed wildlife. Rabbits scurried from bush to bush, small chipmunks with furry gray and white racing stripes running down their backs foraged for nuts and berries, and one afternoon, I spotted a small deer who after a long staring contest with me, leaped elegantly over a fallen tree disappearing in the foliage.

I wandered into a vacant camp with an empty picnic table. Its thick wood turned soft silvery gray from years of exposure to cool, wet rainy days. Rays of sun brightened the leaves of the Ash trees surrounding the camp, lighting them a brilliant green. The forest smelled fresh, like a spring day after it rained. I reveled in the peaceful calm of the forest. The blue sky, gleaming beams of sunlight peeking through the trees, brightening the leaves, was one of the most beautiful sights I'd ever seen.

On Saturday morning of that first week while we were cleaning up after breakfast, Brian, who was the adult in charge of the waterfront, came in and spoke with mom. After a few minutes, he walked to the middle of the kitchen.

"Attention guys. I'm short on staff at the waterfront. One guy was a no show, and you probably heard. I had to send Steven Reeves home for fighting. If you can swim, I could use a few part-time volunteers. If you're interested, report to the waterfront for a swim test in an hour."

Mom shooed Brian out of her kitchen. "Thanks, Brian. I'm sure the boys will be happy to help." Once he was gone, she said, "If he selects you, you'll be on the waterfront most afternoons. That won't leave you much free time. I'll still expect you back here for your kitchen duties."

Working on the waterfront part-time sounded more exciting than serving slop and scrubbing pots full-time. Once we finished cleanup, Eric and I ran to our cabin to change clothes.

We'd all heard that Steve got sent home because he started a fight, but the senior staff kept the details quiet, causing rumors to swirl.

I was pulling on my swim trunks when I said, "Tony told me Steve and Mark fought over a rowboat. Who would do that? There's lots of boats?"

"No, that wasn't it. Tim was there. He told me the whole thing. You'll meet Tim down at the waterfront. Steve didn't like Mark. Tim says Steve knew Mark from juvie. They both spent time at Skipworth. Steve constantly called Mark names, egging him on to fight. Steve bugged Mark for days, but Mark never reacted. When Steve threw the first punch, Mark finally fought back and pounded Steve's ass, totally creamed him. Lucky for Steve, Brian stopped it, or Mark might've killed him."

"Which one of the waterfront guys is Mark?"

"You've seen him. He's the biggest, strongest guy down there. Stay clear of him. He's been arrested before, spent months in juvenile detention. That boy's bad news."

"If he's bad news, why didn't Brian send Mark home?"

"Brian knew it was Steve's fault. Don't worry, Brian's always on Mark's case. You'll see Mark when we get down there. Be careful not to piss him off."

When we arrived at the lake shore, I noticed a group of boys standing outside a large gray canvas tent at the far end of the golden beach. We ran over and joined the group. I stood on my toes looking up at Brian, the waterfront crew, and the other recruits.

Brian had the look of a cool guy in his late twenties. Managing the waterfront of a boy scout camp for the summer was a laid-back job. He was tall and fit, with long, uncombed black hair and a thick two-day beard. I remember staring as he talked, fixated on his bristling facial hair. The individual hairs were thick and black, growing out of deep pores all over his face. How could such thick stubble grow out of his face like that? He wore the waterfront uniform, red baggy shorts, a white t-shirt silk-screened with the Camp Baker logo and white converse tennis shoes. His new wife, Molly, who was very pregnant, accompanied Brian. I felt sorry for her. She spent most of the summer in that old gray tent.

"Listen guys. If you have lifeguard duty, I don't want you doing jack shit," Brian said. We erupted in nervous laughter because an adult had just said the word shit.

When the laughter died down, Rusty, a thin red-headed boy with freckles covering his entire face, asked, "What's jack shit mean?"

"It means doing nothing. Don't do jack shit. Don't look like you're doing nothing," Brian explained.

"I ain't doing jack shit," said Dennis, a fat boy with shaggy brown hair.

Eric chimed in. "Dennis doesn't give a shit." Everyone laughed and the rest of us spouted sentences using the word shit until Brian stopped us. The only boy who had said nothing was a well-tanned muscular guy with black hair who stood silently, watching. He was the strongest boy in the group, so I guessed he was Mark.

"Guys. This is my wife, Molly," Brian said, acknowledging the beautiful young woman with long brown hair flowing gently over her shoulders seated in the tent that functioned as the waterfront headquarters.

"Hi boys. I'm looking forward to spending a wonderful summer with you all."

"Molly will help me manage the waterfront. As you can see, she is very pregnant with our twin boys." Molly smiled as she rubbed her enormous belly.

"Pregnant?" Eric asked.

"We got married in Hawaii. We had sex for the very first time on our wedding night and bang. Instantly pregnant." Brian explained.

Molly smiled. "Amazing how that works."

"Yeah. I'm a stud. An instant baby maker."

She patted her belly. "We are thrilled."

"Yes, we are," Brian nodded. "All right, enough jack shit boys. All the new guys line up at the end of the dock for the swim test. Get moving."

Even though Molly's condition was obvious, the fact that Brian got her pregnant on the first try was a shocking concept. I knew about sex, the mechanics of it anyway, but it never occurred to me that a guy could get a girl pregnant by doing it only once.

I'd learned about sex. They'd taught us in school. We had a single boy's only sex education class one afternoon at the end of the sixth-grade school year. The male teacher played an old film called 'From Boy to Man' for a classroom full of eleven-and twelve-year-old boys. It was about your voice changing, growing hair, and getting erections. There was lots of giggling.

What I didn't learn in that one-hour sex class, I heard from guys talking. I never got a birds and bees talk. My mom never talked to me about sex, and dad was long gone. Like most things in life, I discovered sex on my own.

I ran with the other boys in the warm sun across the sandy shore of Siltcoos lake to wooden docks with white painted planks. The docks floated on large blocks of foam mounted underneath. Each dock was thirty feet long, with a six-inch gap between sections. Each section of dock teeter tottered as we ran from one end of the dock to the next. I remember running across those weathered planks, ever watchful for a raised rusty nail that would hurt like heck if you stepped on one. It was fun to run across the gap between docks, feeling the next section dip under your weight, watching the far end rise, then level off as you ran over the paint chipped boards, dipping again at the far end.

Five sections of dock extended out over the water, secured by a single wood piling at the end where another section of three docks stretched to the right creating an upside-down L. Tied to this section was a line of sailboats, canoes, rowboats, and an old speedboat.

Standing at the end of the docks in the cool breeze absorbing the warmth of the sun, I felt the Oregon dampness being drawn from my soul, burning off the dull gray clouds that fogged my brain. To the north, the shoreline was populated with tall green reeds rising out of the shallow water. I looked across the lake, observing the shimmering sunlight reflecting off the undulating surface, stretching for miles to the south. Transfixed by its vastness; I watched as the coastal wind picked up, whipping the dark green water into small rippling whitecaps.

I stood in line with five other recruits at the end of the dock. Dennis, the fat boy with shaggy hair, had instant authority because he wore the red shorts and white t-shirt of waterfront staff. Dennis walked up and down the line of boys telling us about the lake. "Siltcoos is an Indian word. It means dark and deep. The water is so dark you can't see the bottom. Good thing it's dark because you wouldn't want to see what's down there. This lake is full of sturgeons and eels."

"What are sturgeons?" I asked.

"They're an ugly prehistoric fish with big teeth. Fish dinosaurs."

"Fish dinosaurs? Are you bullshitting us?" Eric asked.

"Get your shirts off and be ready to swim," instructed Tim, a tall boy with blonde hair, wearing red shorts.

"Guess you're about to find out," Dennis said with a cocky grin.

The six of us pulled our t-shirts off and moved to the dock's edge, waiting for Brian. I looked down at the water, trying to see beyond the rippling surface of the dark green water.

Dennis leaned in to tell me more. "The sturgeons' bite isn't the bad part. It's the flesh rotting bacteria on their teeth. I am not shitting you. I heard one boy had his leg amputated from just a small bite."

"Flesh rotting bacteria?" I asked.

"That's right. Oh, one more tip that might save your life. If you're swimming and see a zigzagging ripple on the surface. Swim away as fast as you can. It could be an electric eel."

"Electric eel?"

"Don't worry. They're not actually electric. They call them that because the sting feels like an electric shock. Buzz," Dennis shook his flabby body, making a buzzing sound.

Brian walked up, barking instructions. "This summer we'll have a new group of scouts cycling through each week. They're attending camp to earn merit badges for swimming, rowing, canoeing, and sailing. If I select you to work the waterfront, you will be trained as lifeguards and help instruct classes. Before we train you, I need to know that you can swim. Dennis and Rusty are new to the waterfront staff. Tim and Mark worked last summer. They are senior staff and my assistants, so you guys do what Mark and Tim tell you. Got it."

At sixteen years old, Mark and Tim were older and taller than the rest of the boys. They wore the same red shorts and white t-shirt as Brian, Rusty, and Dennis. Mark stared ahead with brooding eyes. His skin had a dark tan that complemented his muscular body. Everyone else's skin was pale, the result of the sunless Oregon winter. Tim was tall with stringy blonde hair falling into his eyes. His skin was as pasty white as the rest of us.

"I want each of you to jump in the water feet first. Jump. Don't dive. Do you hear me? You will tread water for thirty seconds, swim around the buoy and back to shore. It's about a hundred yards," Brian said pointing to a Clorox bottle painted orange floating fifty yards offshore. "Once you get to shore, run back here. Dennis, show them how it's done, in you go."

Dennis pulled off his shirt, exposing his big flabby belly, took three steps back, then ran and jumped in the air, pulling his knees to his chest yelling, "cannon ball." His blubbery body hit the water, sending up an enormous splash. We all stepped back to avoid getting hit by the tidal wave.

"Bad example Dennis," Brian scolded. "No cannon balls. First in line, jump in."

Bruce, the want to be rock star from our kitchen crew, leaned forward as he jumped, causing him to bellyflop. His body slapped the water loudly when he hit. Everyone cringed. "Ouch. That's got to hurt. Next in line, jump in, feet first," Brian ordered.

Eric jumped in the air with a stylish move, kicking his feet to one side like a kung fu fighter before splashing into the lake and submerging. He surfaced, shaking water from his hair. "Woo, it's cold," he shouted as he tread water.

Tony jumped in normally, his long blond hair splaying out like a white net as he hit the water. "That's a good jump. What's your name?" Brian asked.

"Tony," he shouted back.

I was next. "I want to see a normal jump, just like Tony. No fancy moves. In you go," said Brian. I knew I should've jumped right away, but I froze, feeling the cracked paint beneath my toes transfixed on the dark rippling water, trying to peer through the murk. I could swim, but I had only swum in a pool with clear water and lane lines painted on the bottom.

"Danny, go." I heard Eric yell. The longer I stood, the more panicked I became. I stared down at the black water filled with eels and toe-nibbling dinosaur fish. I wanted to jump but I couldn't move.

"The ditz said he can swim," Eric shouted.

Tim circled around me with a taunting smile. "Is the little boy scared?"

Dennis jerked in the water and screamed. "Ow. A Sturgeon bit me. I'm dying," he drawled as he sank underwater.

I felt a warm stream run down the inside of my thigh and twist around my calf. Just as Tim was saying, "He's pee—." Mark pushed me, sending my body gracelessly into the cold water.

The boys laughed, but Brian was mad. "Mark. Never push anyone into the water. What if he landed on another swimmer or hit his head on the dock?"

As Brian scolded Mark, something out on the lake caught his eye. He stopped yelling and turned to look, just as a sailboat out in the middle of the lake tipped over.

Brian watched the sail and mast go out of sight, revealing the faded blue hull. The boys struggled in the water, unable to right the boat.

A threatening black cloud moved across the sky, darkening the sun. Siltcoos is a coastal lake, less than a mile from the Pacific Ocean. The weather can change fast, as it did that day.

"Those guys told me they knew how to sail. Tim. You're with me. Mark, watch the boys. I'll finish with you later," Brian ordered as he ran to the old speedboat tied to the dock. He fired up the engine as Tim cast off the ropes. The boat raced across the lake with a throaty roar on its way to rescue the sailboat.

Mark scowled at the boys, treading water. "Swim. The rest of you, jump in." The last two boys jumped and began treading water. Dennis, Eric, Tony, and Bruce, the belly flopper, swam for the buoy, but I continued to tread water.

My heart was beating hard, but nothing bit me. I looked up at Mark. I wanted to thank him for saving me from the humiliation of peeing myself, but he was watching the speedboat. Maybe he felt me staring because he turned and saw me treading water. "Can you swim or not?" he scowled. I nodded and began swimming with my head up, unwilling to put my face in the dark green lake.

As we ran to the end of the dock, we watched Brian and Tim rescue the sailboat. The weather was getting worse. The wind whipped the lake surface into larger white caps cresting in turbulent waves. Tim jumped in the water, swam to the sailboat, and put his weight on the high side. Slowly, he lifted the mast and wet sail out of the water. Brian pulled the two boys into the speedboat, then a rope was secured to the sailboat before Tim climbed back into the speedboat.

Brian went to the captain's chair. We heard a pop and saw black smoke cough from the outboard motor. Brian rushed to the rear of the boat, removed the engine cowling, checked something, then moved back to the captain's chair. We saw another puff of black smoke as the wind pushed the two stranded boats further out in the stormy lake.

Mark eyed the row boats tied at the dock. "You guys stay here," he said, running to an old wooden rowboat with several layers of chipped green paint. He untied the boat, sat on the dock, and pulled the boat to him with his feet. Once the boat was broadside to the dock, he jumped in, sat on the middle thwart, and grabbed the oars. He used the blade of one oar to push away from the dock, and then, with the oars in their oarlocks, bent toward the stern, dipped both oars in the water, and pulled hard, propelling the boat forward.

"He's rowing out to them," said Rusty, the redhead.

Eric poked his elbow in my ribs. "Mark's crazy."

"I hope he can save them," I said.

"Mark is crazy. That's why Brian is always on his case. You'll be sorry if you make him angry," Dennis confided.

Mark dug the oars deep in the water, pushing with his legs while pulling with his arms in powerful strokes. Stroke after stroke, Mark powered the old rowboat through the wind and waves until he reached the boats adrift in the middle of the lake.

Tim and another boy were using paddles, trying to move the speedboat. When Mark pulled alongside the stalled boats, we couldn't hear, but we saw Brian standing in the speedboat yelling at Mark.

We wrapped towels over our shoulders as the sky darkened and the wind grew fierce. The end of my towel fluttered in the wind whipping against my leg. I leaned against the wood piling at the end of the dock as the floating platform bucked and rolled under my feet in the choppy water.

Mark tossed a rope to Brian. With the rope secured, Mark rowed. With each stroke, the bow of the small rowboat rose high in the air, then crashed down on two-foot waves, sending a spray of water over the rowboat's bow. We watched as Mark dug the oars deep in the stormy chop, pulling the speedboat, the sailboat, and four passengers. Tim and the other boy continued to paddle from the speedboat, but they weren't helping much. Brian and the second boy sat watching Mark row them through the windswept swells.

Mark rowed stroke after stroke against the raging wind and surf. As the rowboat got closer, I could see muscles in his arms and back straining from the ordeal. After several minutes, he hauled the tethered speedboat and sailboat to the docks looking like a derelict boat parade.

Dennis, Rusty, Eric, the other boys, and I swarmed Mark as he looped a rope around a metal cleat to secure his rowboat. Everyone might be afraid of him, but at that moment we were in awe of Mark and his rowing feat. As he stood before us, with his tangled black hair and beaming smile, the sun broke through the clouds, warming our skin and quieting the wind. Mark's muscled chest and torso, moist with sweat and spray, glistened in the new sunlight. He stood tall and proud, holding out his palms, bloodied by the rough wooden oars for us to see.

Brian burst through the cluster of boys, shaking a scolding finger at Mark. "Never pull a stunt like that again. You could have made a dangerous situation worse."

"Your engine stalled. You were drifting further out," Mark said, his pride deflated.

"It was dangerous and irresponsible."

"You're just mad because you're the one who needed rescuing."

Brian looked embarrassed for a moment, but replied, "I'm angry because you acted without thinking. First you pushed a frightened boy into the water, not knowing if he could swim. He could have drowned, then you pull this rowing stunt."

"He was... Eric said he could swim," Mark stammered.

"If I wasn't short on staff, I'd kick you off the waterfront and have you sent home," Brain chided.

"You can't fire me."

"I sure as hell can fire you. I defended you and sent Steve home. Maybe I should have sent you home, too. Sent you home or wherever they send juvenile delinquents."

"Don't send me back, Brian. Please." It looked like Mark could have cried at that moment. Eric said Mark was bad news. Dennis said he was crazy. I thought it odd for such a strong, daring young man to fear being sent home.

"Your counselor said giving you extra responsibility would help bring you in line. I guess being senior staff isn't enough responsibility, so I'll give you more, but this is your last chance."

"I'll do whatever you say. Just don't send me home."

"You say he can swim," Brian pointed at me. "Now it's your job to make sure he can swim. I don't care if he starts with the dog paddle. He's your responsibility. You're assigned to, what's your name?"

"Danny Novak," I said.

"You're assigned to Danny. You will teach him to swim, row, sail, and canoe and you're responsible for his safety."

"Oh man. Don't stick me with this kid. Punish me with anything else. I'll rake the beach. I'll paint the docks, anything you want," Mark said, negotiating his punishment.

"OK. You'll both rake the beach. You'll do it together. It's Danny's punishment for signing up to work the waterfront when he can't swim and you for these stunts."

"But I swam," I said meekly.

"He did," Eric and Bruce confirmed.

"I didn't see it. I was busy rescuing these two yahoos who said they could sail," Brian snarled at the boys from the sailboat.

"Come on, man. Don't make me waste my summer babysitting some little kid," Mark whined.

I turned to leave. "Screw this. I don't need anyone watching me. Forget the waterfront. I'll just work in the kitchen."

Brian grabbed me by the shoulders and turned me around to face him. "No. You will show up every afternoon and Mark will teach you to swim. If you can finish the mile swim at the end of Jamboree week, that's six weeks from now, you're both off the hook." Brian paused, looking at the other swimmers. "The two boys I saw swim, Tony, and Eric, will help lifeguard during the afternoons. I'll talk to Mom and arrange your schedules. Get moving to the dining hall. It's time for lunch." Brian pointed at Mark, then me. "This afternoon, you two are raking the beach," Brian said, then pushed his way through the group of boys.

Everyone scrambled across the docks, jumped to the beach, and ran up the hill. I hung back, surveying the wide beach. The wind had littered the sand with sticks and pinecones. It would be a long afternoon.

Eric, Tony, and I worked the lunch line serving fish sticks, French fries, and coleslaw. Eric was at the end of the line, spooning globs of moist coleslaw on plates that passed by, "You really screwed up this time, dick weed. All you had to do was jump in. Now everyone's mad at me for saying you could swim."

I scooped four fish sticks off a sheet pan with a spatula and slid them on a plate. "I couldn't stop thinking about what Dennis said."

Tony used tongs to grab fries out of a square steel pan. "Dennis is a jerk."

Eric dug his spoon into the coleslaw. "Mark's pissed. I told you not to piss him off. I hope he's not mad at me."

I scooped six fish sticks, then shook the spatula to drop two back on the pan and served four. "Brian overreacted. Mark was trying to help. Then Brian punishes both of us. It's not fair. I don't even want to work the waterfront anymore."

Tony dropped a pile of fries on a plate. "I don't think you have a choice. I saw Brian talking to Mom. Eric and I are working on the waterfront, too."

"Yeah, but you're not stuck with Mark," I said, sliding fish sticks on a plate.

"All you had to do was jump," Eric said, digging a heaping spoonful of slaw.

After lunch, I grabbed a rake I found near the tent. Molly sat nearby in the shade of a tree, reading a book. She watched as I raked, working my way across the beach to the docks. The rake had long rusty tines, several of them were missing like broken teeth, letting debris pass through the gaps, making the job of smoothing out the sand and raking up trash more challenging.

Mark walked past without acknowledging me, grabbed another rake, then walked to the far end of the beach. He dragged his rake through the sand, stopping every time he found a pinecone to throw it into the forest.

I raked sticks, pinecones, and trash into small piles. Each sweep of my rake and step forward brought Mark and me closer. Mark didn't look at me as we raked past each other. He swept his rake and stepped forward; his eyes fixed on his bare feet. "Keep away from me, punk.

You ruined my summer," he said, then kicked a pile of sticks and trash into the line I had just raked.

His words hurt. I'd imagined being stuck with the same sucky punishment might bring us together, like friends. It was clear he didn't want to be friends, so I increased the speed of my raking and ignored him.

I worked at a determined pace to finish my punishment as fast as possible. When I had raked two-thirds of the beach and dumped my trash piles into a rusty oil barrel, I presented myself to Molly. "I raked more than half. Can I go? I'm supposed to be in the kitchen.

"You can go. I'll tell Brian you did more than your share."

Mark looked up from his drudgery and flipped me off as I ran past him. I paused for a moment, then ran up the hill, away from the waterfront.

Chapter Five

Boy Scouts flooded the camp, chasing away the peaceful calm of the forest. Sitting on the steps of the dining hall that Sunday morning, I watched three hundred scouts, and their adult leaders march into camp like an invading force. Boys of all shapes and sizes aged from eleven to seventeen ready for fun and the adventure of a lifetime sent clouds of dust rising over the main trail as waves of stomping feet and backpacks tromped past.

The scout troops had received their camp assignments before arriving, but it was still a sight to watch Scoutmasters herd their boys to campsites. The main trail became a busy thoroughfare of boys exploring old forest trails, running down smaller paths that led to camps with names like Arrowhead, Heceta, and Conestoga, past the nature and ecology buildings, the scout craft area, all the way to the archery range near the end of the peninsula.

Most of that first week, I was stuck working in the kitchen anchored at the sink cleaning pots except for the times the cook staff asked me to work the serving line scooping eggs, lasagna, or mashed potatoes onto faceless plates filing past.

The best thing about working at the sink were the windows with a view of the grassy assembly area. I would gaze out and daydream about a better life while scrubbing. Watching scouts enjoy the sunshine, run through the grass, chase after each other, or play Frisbee made me yearn to be outside. I didn't mind working. I needed the money, but I couldn't help imagining being carefree, running through the forest or canoeing all day.

Most boys had fathers who paid for everything. I wasn't that lucky. It was easy to spot the boys with new boots purchased for a week at camp wearing nicely pressed uniforms with all the patches carefully sewed on by their mother. The happy-looking boys with new haircuts. I tried not to envy them.

I was used to toiling, making my own way. Money at home was tight, and I hated asking my mother for anything, fearing she'd yell at me reciting her familiar rants. Money didn't grow on trees and my dad was a dead-beat who never sent enough money. If I wanted to buy something, I'd earn the money picking weeds, mowing lawns, or delivering newspapers and pay for it myself.

Sometimes, as daylight faded after dinner, I imagined I worked in the galley of a slave ship. Chained to the sink, I scoured black pots caked with crusty dried gruel, hoping that pirates would board the ship and set me free. Then I'd join the rogues sailing the seven seas in search of gold and jewels. I often dreamed of being rescued, lifted out of my of drudgery, but no one ever came.

Working in the kitchen was not fun. I was used to working, but the other boys acted like work was a fatal disease. We were supposed to have breaks between breakfast and lunch. We should have the afternoons off, but we had almost no free time. After what happened the last time I complained, I held my tongue, focused on scrubbing pans and looking out the window, daydreaming about a better life.

During that first week of campers, I only made it to the waterfront twice. I was supposed to spend my afternoons basking in the sun, swimming, learning to row, paddle, and sail, but the kitchen crew spent most of our time in the kitchen.

Late one afternoon I marched across the docks wearing my baggy black swim trunks with a towel tucked under my arm, only to find that Mark had taken a group of boys rowing. I sat on the dock with my feet dangling in the water, hoping he'd come back before I had to return for kitchen duty. No matter what I'd said, I wanted to be part of the waterfront staff more than anything. I wanted those red shorts and the white t-shirt. I wanted to be part of the coolest, most respected group of staff at camp. All I had to do was prove to Mark that I could swim so Brian would let me work the waterfront.

A group of boys ran across the dock, headed for the beach. Rusty yelled after them as he struggled with their sailboats, the sails fluttering in the wind. Rusty was having a hard time securing the boats, so I ran over. "Tell me what to do. I'll help."

Following Rusty's instructions, we lowered the sails, pulled out the dagger boards, and removed the rudders on three sailboats. As we worked, I noticed that freckles covered Rusty's entire body. His back, chest, and legs, all freckled. It was as if God couldn't decide if the boy should have a nice tan or stay completely white. When we finished, Rusty thanked me, then went off to assist some other boys. Looking out across the lake, I spotted the rowboats in the distance. Mark wasn't coming back.

On my second visit to the waterfront, I spotted Mark on the dock by the rowboats and canoes. I ran across the sand and jumped on the first section of dock. I ran past Tim, who was kneeling on the white planks next to a red toolbox, hammering down loose nails.

Mark saw me and scurried into a canoe paddling away before I got to the end of the dock. Screw him, I thought. I wasn't the one who'd get sent home if I couldn't finish the mile swim. He was the one who was in trouble. It wasn't my fault that Brian made me Mark's punishment.

The sharp sound of Tim's hammer hitting the planks echoed across the water. I walked back across the docks with my head down, spotting rusty nails poking above the boards. When I reached Tim, I saw a second hammer in the toolbox. I dropped my towel, reached for the hammer, knelt, and started hammering. Tim glanced over at me, then went back to hammering. We worked silently side by side to the meditative sound, ping, ping, ping, ping, knocking nails down plank by plank.

The way things were going, it looked like our cleanup crew would spend most of the summer in the kitchen.

We were disorganized, and everyone worked slowly. It took us almost three hours to clean up after lunch and we worked until nine o'clock each night after dinner. I was upset because we missed all the evening activities. It really pissed me off when we missed Friday night's big campfire. Campfire was the week's main event, with skits, music, an awards ceremony, and a huge bonfire. It was the grand finale before the campers went home Saturday morning after breakfast.

That night, I'd finished my pots and pans early and helped the others so we could get out of the kitchen sooner, but we still finished late. I was at camp to work, but I didn't want to work eighteen hours a day. I knew if I spoke up, I might suffer the consequences, but I couldn't take it anymore.

Finally, I yelled at everybody. "Come on, guys. We need to work smarter. You can load me up with all the scummy pots you want for saying this, but we need to work as a team. Unless you want to spend your entire summer in this kitchen?"

Eric threw a dirty white towel on a table. "It's not my fault everybody works slow."

I felt encouraged. "We can do better. We're missing out on all the fun."

James stepped to Eric. "It shouldn't take three hours to wipe down the tables. Everyone works faster than you."

"I want to have fun this summer, don't you guys?" I asked.

Eric picked up the towel and snapped James in the ass with it. The towel made a loud crack. James jumped and howled. "I'm all about having fun," Eric said.

James threatened to punch Eric. "Screw you. You're the laziest one here."

"Come on, guys. If we work as a team, we'll finish sooner and have more free time. From now on, let's help each other and work faster. If we do that, we'll get out of here earlier."

Tony stopped mopping the floor. "I'd love getting out of here earlier."

Kurt shoved a load of plates into the Beast. "He might be a runt, but the kids got a point." Everyone looked at Kurt. Those were the most words we'd heard him speak since we'd met him.

Bruce, wearing a Led Zeppelin t-shirt, brushed his long black hair out of his face. "How would this work?"

Eric walked toward me, spinning his towel into a lethal weapon. "Yeah, Novak. Let's hear your great idea for getting us out of here faster."

"First, Kurt can operate the Beast and stack the clean dishes while the Beast washes the next load. That frees up Bruce so the four of you, can wipe down the dining tables and benches faster. Then two people sweep the floor followed by two people mopping. You'll have the dining hall cleaned in thirty minutes instead of two hours, then you move into the kitchen cleaning as a team. I bet we can get out of here an hour faster. What do you guys say?"

James looked at the other guys, checking their reactions. "I suppose you expect us to help you scrub pots."

"Nope. You can help put the clean pans away, but I'll do all the scrubbing. Does that sound fair?"

"Novak's a friggin efficiency expert," Eric cheered.

Mom must have heard us talking. As the guys hustled to finish up, she stepped out of her office and walked over to me. She spoke in a low voice. "Didn't I say you'd be running with the pack? What I didn't know is that you'd be the leader." She winked at me and shuffled back to her office.

Me, a leader? I didn't know what to think about that. I just wanted to get the job done and have some fun.

After that night, we worked as a team and finished cleaning up faster after every meal, giving us time for relaxing breaks between breakfast and lunch, most of our afternoons free, and we never missed a campfire the rest of Summer.

Chapter Six

My scout troop from home arrived Sunday morning for a week at camp. I planned to visit them, but first I made my trek to the waterfront, ever hopeful that Mark would fulfill his obligation.

As I walked down the hill to the beach with my backpack slung over one shoulder, I saw at least seventy boys splashing in the water. I didn't realize that on the first day new campers arrive, most of them go to the waterfront.

Dennis and Rusty were lifeguarding from the dock, while Tony was blowing his whistle and shouting at the boys from the beach. Mark helped boys launch rowboats, canoes, and the two-man sail boats. Brian and Tim were out in the speedboat chasing after boaters that went out too far. It was controlled chaos.

I saw Molly sitting in her chair on the beach. I walked over and plopped down on the sand next to her. "Looks like a busy day on the waterfront."

"It's crazy daze. The first afternoon of the week is always out of control. Classes start tomorrow. It will be calmer then."

"I should be out there with Tony, but Brian won't let me work until Mark tells him I can swim. Every time I approach Mark, he paddles away. He hates me."

"Give Mark time. He'll come around."

I wanted to work on the waterfront, but I didn't want to sound desperate. "I'm not worried. He's not my punishment," I said, laying back. "I came to work on my tan," I said, pulling my pack under my head for a pillow.

Lying on my back with my eyes closed, I imagined myself swimming in the lake. If Mark gave me the chance, I would swim. I had swum before.

━━━━━━━

My mind wandered back to three summers' before at the city's indoor pool, when I had learned to swim. I remembered how kids' voices and water splashing echoed off the ceiling and walls of the enclosed space and I remembered the young lifeguard, Quinn. He was a handsome guy in his early twenties with frizzy chlorine bleached blonde hair and a funny crooked smile that showed his vampire teeth. Sometimes he taught the group that my younger brother Billy was in, other times he sat in the tall lifeguard chair.

One afternoon, the woman that taught my group had us kids sit on the edge of the pool to practice our breaststroke frog kick. I saw my mom on the other side of the pool talking with Quinn. While I frog kicked, I watched them go into the boiler room. They were in there for a long time.

I was curious, so after the lesson, I opened the boiler room door and looked inside. It was a humid, dimly lit room with a big tank connected to a bunch of pipes. My mom and Quinn went into the boiler room several times that summer. As a kid, I never understood what they found so interesting in that musty room.

The city's swim club planned to hold a swim meet at the end of summer. I must have been doing well because the coach approached my mom. He said I had potential and recommended that I join the swim team. Billy asked if he had potential, too. The coach told Billy swimming might not be his sport. I thought the coach's reply was funny. Billy threw a fit. I trained with the swim team for the rest of the summer.

The day of the swim meet, I was surprised to see my dad show up in time for my last event. I was excited to see him; he must have left work early to watch me swim. I stood on the starting block clapping my hands, getting myself pumped for the race. Most kids went through the motions of racing without conviction. This was a swim meet, a competition. To me, that meant I was supposed to race and try my best to win. I swam my heart out and won my heat. I was excited and looked for my dad, but he wasn't watching. He was marching rapidly across the pool deck toward the boiler room door, where Quinn stood with my mother in his arms. There was lots of yelling.

That night my parents were fighting so loud I couldn't sleep. I got out of bed, cracked the bedroom door open, and listened. "I can't take it, Darlene. I show up and you're being groped by some teenage lifeguard."

"Quinn's not a teenager. Don't worry, he means nothing to me."

"You did this at the pool where every mother in town could see you. People talk, Darlene. Wives tell their husbands. How's this supposed to make me look? I can't even control my own wife."

"It's over. I'll never see him again." I knew that was probably true. It was the end of summer. After the swim meet, the pool closed for the season.

"I can't live like this, Darlene. You said this wouldn't happen again. Is Billy even mine?"

"Why are you bringing that up again? Of course, Billy's your boy. How dare you think that? Nothing happened, baby. You're getting worked up over nothing."

Billy heard his name and snuggled next to me at the door. "What are they arguing about?"

"Nothing, go back to bed." I closed the door so he couldn't hear.

"Is dad mad at me? I get scared when they fight."

"It's not your fault. Go to sleep."

I could see why my dad would wonder about Billy. Both mom and dad had blond hair. My dad was tall and wiry. Mom was shapely and attractive. I was thin with dirty blond hair. Billy was short, stocky, had a pug nose, and dark brown hair. People said he'd be a football player or a boxer. As brothers go, there was no family resemblance.

I peeked out the door again.

"You'll never change. You were a slut when I met you, and you're still a lying whore."

Smack. Mom slapped dad. "A real man would know how to satisfy his woman."

"I'm not putting up with your bullshit. It's over, Darlene." Dad left the house, slamming the door.

My parents divorced shortly after that. Dad moved out, and I didn't swim again until Mark pushed me off the dock.

━━━━━━━━━━

I sat up, gazing at the lake, digging my toes in the sand, feeling the heat of the sun on my skin. Mark was out in his rowboat monitoring the other boats. He didn't have time for me, but today it wasn't his fault.

I hung out on the beach chatting with Molly and later joined a game of beach football. It felt great to run and play, feeling the hot sand under my feet. After the game, I changed clothes and went to visit the guys from my scout troop.

I ran up the hill until I reached a trail cutting through a thick blanket of huckleberry shrubs and fern shaded by tall Douglas fir trees. Glossy tree roots crisscrossed the trail, their bark long ago scuffed away by hundreds of boot treads. The huckleberry shrubs had thick sturdy leaves and dark purple berries, which I didn't dare eat. I never learned if they were poisonous.

Tyee camp sat on a bluff overlooking Siltcoos lake. The camp had four Adirondack shelters, a fire pit, and a Scoutmaster's cabin set away from the shelters. An Adirondack is a three-sided shelter, open in the front, with a cement floor. Wooden bunks lined two walls with beds for four scouts.

As I approached the camp, I noticed a piece of twine stretched across the trail. A trip wire. I stepped carefully over the taut, fibrous cord. Several feet ahead, a wooden gate assembled from branches lashed together with twine blocked the trail. I noticed a large pinecone hanging from another piece of twine next to the gate. I grabbed the pinecone, pulled it hard, and heard a bonk, the distinctive tone of wood striking the bottom of a metal cooking pot. "Who goes there?" asked a voice from inside the camp.

"It's me. Danny," I called out. Someone in camp pulled a long piece of the ever-present twine and the gate swung open. As I entered the camp, I saw boys from my troop eagerly weaving a roll of twine around trees fencing the perimeter of Tyee camp. A boy named Jeff sat hunched over, sitting on a rock, concentrating on his work. I watched as he placed a huckleberry leaf on a stump, cut the leaf in half along its thick center vein, then guided the leaf into a groove he'd cut into a foot-long stick. He sealed the leaf in place with narrow strips of gray duct tape.

"Is that an arrow?" I asked.

"It will be," he said as he spun the makeshift arrow between his fingers, now with three fletchings installed. He dipped the pointy end into a tin can at the edge of a small fire. When he extracted it, black sticky goo covered the tip. "It's pitch," he said, waving the stick and its acrid fumes in the air to cool the black tar. He then shaped the sticky glob with his fingers. Once he'd secured the pitch on the tip, he rested the shaft on his index finger to check the arrow for balance.

Jeff mounted the makeshift arrow into a crossbow he had fashioned out of freshly cut branches and more twine. He pulled the arrow back, stretching the twine tight, and locked the string into a notch, arming the bow. Jeff lowered his pimple covered face to examine his craftmanship. "If the guys from the other camp try to raid us tonight, we'll be ready for them," Jeff announced.

A young boy named Brent ran up to Jeff. "We have tons of pinecones stashed at the artillery positions. If they attack, we'll wipe them out." Brent was a chubby blonde kid who had gained fame in our troop for using a lighter to ignite his farts.

Mr. Holman, our Scoutmaster, stepped out of his cabin and strode across the camp. "Hey Danny, how's life as camp staff? Are they treating you alright?"

"It's OK. The work isn't too hard and most of the guys are cool. I thought I'd stop by to see how you guys are doing."

"Apparently, the boys are preparing for battle."

To me, it was natural that the boys played war. For as long as I could remember, the six o'clock news broadcast the Vietnam war into America's living rooms every night, often displaying violent battle footage. Boys in our troop had older brothers or cousins that had been over there. Some never came back.

Mr. Holman cupped his hands around his mouth and yelled. "Dining hall in five minutes. We walk up together as a troop."

Mr. Holman eyed Jeff's crossbow. "Jeff, you better make sure you don't hurt anybody with your arrows and booby traps. That could take an eye out."

"Nah, it's a dummy," Jeff pointed at the blunt pitch covered end. "It won't hurt anybody, and it's aimed low."

"We'll shock the enemy with our superior weapons," said Brent.

"It's meant to scare them off if they try to raid us," Jeff added. He jerked a piece of twine, releasing the arrow. It shot with a whoosh across camp, bouncing off a tree trunk.

"Wow. You're a genius," I said, admiring Jeff's ingenuity and contraption making skills. Mr. Holman looked cautiously impressed.

A few minutes later, Mr. Holman had corralled a dozen young scouts and got us moving up the trail.

The doors of the dining hall swung open and hundreds of hungry boys pressed through the entrance, running to their assigned tables.

I had the night off from kitchen duty. Mr. Donaldson assigned the members of the camp staff to sit at a different table for each meal, but I got to sit with my troop. Scoutmasters and other adults sat together at tables near the fireplace.

Mr. Donaldson, the head of the senior staff, stood in front of the large fireplace. He made announcements, then dismissed one table at a time to join the cafeteria line. We slid our food trays across a Formica countertop with raised metal rails. There was no soda. The kitchen served milk in eight-ounce wax paper cartons at every meal. Once we had our food, we made our way back to the table.

It felt comfortable surrounded by the guys who knew me. The table was full of happy boys talking and joking as we ate.

Mackey, a chubby-faced boy with plump rosy cheeks, spoke loudly to get everyone's attention. "Hey guys, watch me drink milk through my nose." Mackey's offer caused the table to quiet. All eyes were on Mackey. The boys answered his proposal with taunts like. "Do it." "You're gonna puke."

But the chant, "do it, do it, do it," won out. I admit; I got swept up in the excitement, wondering if Mackey could really drink milk through his nose.

"Prepare to be amazed," Mackey said with a smirk. He hesitated and received more raucous encouragement before using his finger to press one nostril closed and lowered his head, aiming his other nostril over a paper straw. As he lowered his head, it looked like half the straw went up his nose, then he blew milk bubbles. Frothy white domes rose out of the creased diamond shaped opening of the milk carton. The boys responded with laughter and derision. "Faker." "Come on, do it. Do it, do it, do it."

Mackey lifted his head with a panicked look on his round face. "I'm scared."

"He's gonna gag," said Sean, one of the younger boys.

It took little inducement for Mackey to make a second attempt. He lowered his head, sticking the straw up his nostril, and blew bubbles again, drawing scorn. "Cheater." "Come on, man. You said you'd do it."

Without hesitation, Mackey inhaled. I watched the silhouette of milk being drawn up through the straw. When he ran out of breath, Mackey tilted his head back like he was trying to stop a bloody nose. He attempted to let the milk flow into his gullet. Instead of swallowing the milk, he gagged and coughed, splattering milk on everyone.

The long wooden bench filled with boys scooched back, scraping loudly across the tile floor as we tried to evade the spray of snot mixed milk. The table erupted in panicked laughter.

I stood laughing with the bench behind my knees, wiping splotches of milk off my arms and face as I looked around the room. Everyone in the dining hall was looking to see what was happening at our table.

Everyone but Mark. I scanned the grand old hall, seeing boys laughing with all eyes on us. Except Mark, who stared forward, oblivious to the commotion. He must have felt me staring at him because he turned his head slowly until his burning glare met my laughing eyes. Without emotion, he turned away. My laugh faltered. I stared at him, suddenly feeling alone and embarrassed. The bench moved forward, jolting me from my daze, forcing me to sit. Surrounded by the wild boys, all I could think about was the mess Mackey had made. Milk spattered for James and Eric to wipe off the table and milk on the floor that Tony would mop up.

Chapter Seven

After dinner, as the boys streamed out of the hall, I hung back acting like I was helping cleanup, but I was watching Mark. When Mark left the building, I waited, peering out the dining hall window, watching as he marched across the assembly field, past the flagpole, then disappearing into the dark tunnel of trees.

I gave chase, rushing down the broad wooden steps of the dining hall and scurrying across the grass covered assembly area. When I reached the trees, I slowed, allowing my eyes to adjust to the dark and hid behind a tree. Mark was ahead, walking down a side trail leading deeper into the old forest. *Why was I following him?* I asked myself. Everyone warned me about Mark. He'd been arrested, spent time in juvie. He was bad news. I should have turned back. He had avoided me, but I felt compelled to follow.

Imagining I was an Indian boy tracking a deer, I moved stealthily from tree to tree, remaining unseen by my quarry. I advanced, watching the ground to ensure my footsteps would be silent. Deftly, I moved from one large tree to the next. Once in position, I glanced around the thick trunk to view the trail, but Mark was no longer in sight.

I tiptoed to another tree and edged slowly around the trunk to look down the trail, but still, there was no Mark. When I inched back to conceal myself, I hit something. Startled, I spun around, filled with fear, and found Mark standing over me, tall, fierce, and strong.

He pushed me against the tree and scowled, "Quit following me, idiot."

I stared at his angry face, a square jaw and smooth brown skin over high cheekbones, dark hairs on his upper lip, the whisper of a teen's mustache under his wide nose, and jet-black eyes that seemed to pierce through me. The rough tree bark dug into my skin as he pressed harder.

"I wasn't following you," my voice squeaked.

"I saw you sneaking through the forest, spying. Keep away from me, runt."

"Brian said you're supposed to help me swim."

"That doesn't mean you can stalk me like a weird little freak."

"Why are you such an ass? It's not my fault Brian has it out for you."

Mark's face filled with angst, and his nostrils flared as he squashed my body harder against the tree. Mark was powerful. He must have considered me a weak, puny kid. He controlled me so easily. I thought he was about to punch me, but he just pushed me painfully against that old tree.

It was hard to breathe, but I rasped out the words. "I think what you did that day was heroic. Even if Brian was mad that you rescued him."

Mark eased the pressure but still held me. "Yeah, like my uncle used to say, no good deed goes unpunished." He then dropped me and walked away.

I stood unsteadily on the tree's roots, calling after him. "See you tomorrow?"

"Not if I can help it."

How could I be so stupid? Why had I followed him? I'm a child. No wonder he wants nothing to do with me. My head pounded, drumming beats of humiliation. What an idiot, a freak. Ashamed, I had to get away, escape.

I ran as fast as I could in the darkening twilight down a narrow trail that cut across the peninsula, weaving around giant trees, pushing through waist high fern fronds, vaulting over giant roots, and scrambling over fallen trees. I ran through huckleberry bushes clawing at my ankles until I reached the main trail that led down the center of the peninsula. My body ached. I was crushed. How could I ever face him again? I'd snuck around like a little kid and got caught. What a fool, a weird little freak, a runt.

Once my feet found the thick wood chips of the main trail, I slowed my pace, walking with my head down, trying to be invisible to other boys on the trail. I passed trails that led to camps with names like Tsisqan, Captain Gray, and Conestoga. The further I walked, the narrower the trail became, and the fewer scouts I saw until I walked alone.

I went down the path to the Archery Range. The area was empty and quiet. I went to the storage shed and pulled on the padlock, but it didn't give. Jack had locked the bows and arrows inside. I stood on the range, holding my arms in position, imagining I held a bow. I pulled my arm back slowly, flexing the imaginary bowstring, drawing back a deadly arrow until my right hand was on my cheek, aiming the poisonous tip at the vision of my freakishly skinny body. When I released the lethal arrow, I ran across the grass to the paper target mounted on an upright bale of hay.

I stood before the ragged target punctured by a hundred death dealing arrows filled with shame, biting my lower lip. I punched the target with my right hand, then punched it with my left, feeling the texture of the paper target and the straw flexing behind it. Lowering my chin, I punched again and again, hitting the target rapidly like a boxer pummeling a punching bag until I was out of breath. Exhausted, I fell forward with my arms around the bale, breathing hard with sweat beading on my forehead inhaling the hay's earthy smell.

Darkness descended on the peninsula as I walked back up the main trail, brushing pieces of hay from my shirt and jeans. Hay dust stuck to my sweating flesh, causing my arms and face to itch. I rubbed sore knuckles as I walked. My aches and itches, reminders of the childish demon named Danny whom I battled.

Chapter Eight

Walking aimlessly into the camp lit by yellow lights drooping between trees and the sound of Queen's 'We Will Rock You' echoing through the grove stirred me from my morose depression the dark forest allowed. I wiped my eyes and wore a cheery face before walking into the dim light.

A group of boys sat at the picnic table arguing about a card game. Mark was there holding cards close to his chest, yelling at the others to keep playing. I avoided eye contact and veered away from the table, hoping not to be seen, taking a longer route to my cabin.

The Asian boy I'd seen on the first day and two other boys sat on logs around a roaring fire pit playing guitars, singing along with Freddy Mercury. Other staff members ran from one cabin to the next, doors banging shut behind them. The festive mood of the camp did little to lift me from my solitary meditation.

As I walked up the steps to our cabin, Eric burst out the door, almost knocking me over. "Hey, where've you been?"

"Walking."

"Everyone's going to Dennis' cabin. He's got a TV and a videotape machine."

"I'm kinda tired."

"Don't be a lame ass. Why are you always a downer? You gotta learn to have fun, twerp," he said, shaking me by the shoulders.

"What movie are you guys watching?"

Eric leaned in close. "We're gonna watch a porno. You don't want to miss this, dork."

"Porno?" I'd never heard the word. The small town of Lebanon had sheltered me from the world. I'd seen nude pictures in a magazine once when Doug Hansen stole a Hustler magazine from his dad. He showed it to a group of us neighborhood boys in his backyard shed one afternoon.

"Get real. Oh, I forgot you're still a baby. Pornography. A porno movie. Hot naked chicks with huge knockers."

"You mean titties?"

"Man, do I have to teach you everything? You don't call them titties, nimrod. Shit. Where have you been all your life? You call 'em boobs, knockers, chi chi's, melons, jugs, bazoomas, or sweater stretchers, but never call 'em titties."

Eric's enthusiasm lifted my spirits.

"Let's go see some nuga-nuga's."

"Now you're getting it. We'll see so many ginormous bouncing betties, your balls will burst," Eric said, with his hands exploding over his crotch.

I ran with Eric to Dennis' cabin. As the door opened, we were bathed in purple hues from a fluorescent black-light and the haunting sounds of Pink Floyd's Dark Side of the Moon. I felt as if I'd been transported to an alternate reality. As I stumbled in; my mouth agape, staring at glowing posters of psychedelic multicolored magic mushrooms and a naked woman with butterfly wings.

Tim and Rusty lounged on the bottom bunk. James sat on the top bunk, letting his long legs dangle while Dennis kneeled in front of a small portable TV sitting on a videotape machine.

Tim looked to see who'd come in. "Ah, why'd you bring him? He got Mark in trouble. He'd better not squeal on us."

Eric pushed me forward. "He's cool. Well, he will be."

"Be cool," Eric whispered to me.

James rolled on his side and looked down at us. "You sure he's old enough? I bet he doesn't even know all the four-letter words."

Tim started spouting four-letter words, "You mean like dick, tits, suck, fu—."

"I know the 'c' word; but I'm not sure what it means," I said, interrupting Tim.

The boys erupted in wild laughter.

Eric punched my shoulder. "Don't say stupid shit."

"I didn't know," I replied in a whisper.

"Eric, you sure he's not gonna faint when he sees some sex action?" asked James.

Rusty sat up on the edge of the lower bunk. "Play the tape, Dennis. Let Danny see what the 'c' word means."

Dennis held up a VHS tape. "Sexy Nurses Volume One, from my cousin's private collection."

Eric sat on the bunk, nudging Rusty.

Rusty scooted over. "It looks like your cousin has watched that tape a hundred times."

"Why does it look sticky? What's your cousin been doing with that?" asked Tim.

Eric joined in. "Where's he been putting that thing?" The boys laughed again.

James rubbed his groin with exaggerated motions. "Just play the video. I'm ready for action."

Dennis inserted the black plastic rectangle into the wide mouth of the VCR and the eight-inch black-and-white TV screen came to life.

"Keep it in your pants, James. I gotta warn ya, this one is good," Dennis said, pushing Eric aside to squeeze in next to Rusty on the bunk.

Eric pushed Dennis. "How do you know Dennis? You never get past the first five minutes."

"At least I last five minutes, not like you, the one-minute wonder."

Eric pushed Dennis harder. Dennis rolled on Rusty, pushing him on to Tim, and the four boys wrestled on the bunk while the introduction played. I sat on the wood floor; my eyes glued to the small gray screen.

I had a boner before the first scene played. The idea, the anticipation that I was about to watch something sexy, set me off. Lately it seemed almost anything could make me instantly hard. All it took was a thought, or a slight breeze and boing. It was out of control. My dick had a mind of its own. I'd started wearing my shirts untucked to hide it, knowing the thing was apt to pop-up at the most embarrassing moment.

The opening scene featured a busty nurse hovering over a man on an examination table. She unbuttoned the man's shirt, then placed her ear on his bare chest, listening to his heart. The man grabbed the nurse's huge breasts, massaging them. She looked into the man's eyes. "Oh my, your heart is racing. I'd better check your blood pressure." The nurse rose, unbuttoned, and unzipped the man's pants. "I thought you check blood pressure with a cuff around my arm." The man said.

"I prefer my method." The nurse then gripped his manhood. "Oh my, so hard, and big like a stallion."

The image on the TV became jagged lines and electronic noise as the video went out of synch. We groaned in unison.

"What happened?" asked Rusty.

"Where's the boobs, man?" I shouted.

Dennis scooted off the bunk and rushed to the videotape machine. "Hold on. It's just the tracking. I can fix it," he said, adjusting a small dial.

"Just as it was getting good," said Eric.

"I thought you already shot your wad," said Tim.

The picture didn't improve, no matter which direction Dennis turned the knob.

"Maybe you should eject it," said James.

Rusty looked up at James. "The way you were shaking the bunk up there, I thought you were about to eject."

"At least I jerk up here in private, not like you faggots down there."

Dennis pushed the button to eject the tape. The mechanism made a grinding sound and spit the tape out. Dennis pulled the cassette from the slot along with a jumbled mess of brown tape.

"Shit. I forgot to press stop first," Dennis said, clumsily pulling the shimmering brown tape like loose spaghetti.

"You ruined it," said Rusty.

"It pays to finish fast, boys. I'm outta here," Tim said, getting off the bunk.

I sat on the floor laughing as Dennis tried to wind the tape back into the cassette.

Eric scooted off the bed. "Come on Danny. Party's over."

"We'll continue his sex education another time," said James.

Later that night, after Eric had finished his nightly whacking off session, and fallen asleep. I laid in bed thinking about Brenda Rose. Oh, sweet Brenda Rose. She was very cute and had golden hair that seemed to glow. She carried herself with a confident, casual energy. Her personality attracted people without effort. Brenda was nice to everybody, including me. Every morning when I passed her in the hall at school, she'd say, "Good morning, Danny," with a bright smile.

That's all she had to say to take my breath away. "Hi Brenda," I'd gasp. I had a huge crush on her and was desperate that we be friends, at least to say more than good morning, but a group of kids always surrounded her. I was too shy to approach. She already had tons of friends, and she said good morning to everybody. Even though she was special to me, there was no way I would ever be special to her.

One morning Brenda was chatting and laughing with her friends across the hall while I stood next to my locker anxiously, trying to convince myself to be brave and join the group. After staring down, studying my muddy black converse, I looked up and Brenda was looking at me. When she saw me look, she smiled and waved. My heart melted.

I imagined we were alone together, and we kissed. She let me unbutton her blouse, exposing her firm breasts, and I exhaled her name slowly. "Brenda." My bunk was creaking. I was making noise, doing it too hard, but I didn't care. "Ahh, ahh, ahh. Oh, man," I whispered panting.

Eric clapped, then roared. "Thank God. Finally. He choked the chicken, beat the bishop, charmed the cobra, flogged the dong. Danny Novak pounded his meat. He's a human being after all. Maybe now you won't be so uptight."

Embarrassed, I scrambled to pull my shorts up. "You were asleep."

"Until you started rocking around the clock. Creak, creak, creak. I think your bunk has a few loose nails. Who's Brenda?"

"Oh God. Did I say her name out-loud?"

"Oh yeah, you were in the groove. Who is she?"

"A girl from school."

"Yeah, I guessed that. Is she your girlfriend?"

"No."

"I have a girlfriend, Sherry. When I take her to the movies, we sit in the top row and kiss through the entire show. One time we double dated with my buddy Doug. He's got a car. We went to the drive-in. Man, that was a total make-out session. Have you ever made out with a girl?"

"Not yet."

"I forgot, you're still a kid. Don't worry, you'll get there. The girls will like ya. You're not bad looking for a runt."

"Yeah? Sorry I woke you up."

"No, it's great. I was worried about you. Thought you might explode if you didn't do it soon. You need to loosen up, live a little."

"I'm not like you. I like my privacy."

"It's no big deal. Everybody does it, no matter what they try to make you believe. The ones that say they don't are the fucked-up ones. I say let it loose baby."

"And you do, loudly every night."

Eric felt like a big brother teaching me about life and the world, but I was always wary of him as well because at any moment he could cut you knife deep with just a few words.

Chapter Nine

A cloud of humiliation hung over me from my encounter with Mark the night before, but that didn't stop me. I wouldn't say it was a conscious decision. Maybe I lacked the social norms not to tread where I wasn't welcome. Did I have a defect that dulled my senses? Was I infected with a parasite making me advance toward danger, ignoring fear? Oblivious to how others felt, I focused on myself and what I wanted. I was determined to achieve my goal of working on the waterfront, and I would not allow my fear of Mark stop me.

I ran on the main trail until I reached the path leading downhill to the lake. It was a beautiful, sunny day. I paused and looked up. The air smelled fresh, the sky was a brilliant blue, with billowy clouds being pushed over the lake by the cool coastal breeze.

I ran down the hill, across the warm golden sand, then leapt onto the white planks of the dock. I slowed my pace when I spotted Mark sitting at the end of the dock with his back to me, holding an oar. The oar rested in an oar lock mounted on a vertical piece of wood, a device used to teach rowing. Four rowboats filled with two boys each floated on the placid water near the dock.

I tread slowly, watching Mark demonstrate the proper parts of a stroke, the catch, drive, and recovery.

"Feather the oar by rolling your wrist backwards to prepare for the next catch and drive. Then recover and feather again. You guys try it."

I stood silently behind Mark, watching the boys clumsily move their oars. Mark turned suddenly, causing me to jump back. He eyed me, standing uneasily in my baggy black swim shorts. "Shit. The runt came back."

I stepped toward him with trepidation. He held his hand up. "Wait."

Mark looked at the boys in the boats. "You guys take turns rowing, but don't go out too far. Remember to feather your oars."

Mark walked to his rowboat, untied the bowline, and climbed in.

I stood on the dock watching. He'd avoided me every day so far. It didn't look like today would be different. "Are you running away again?" I asked.

The rowboat bumped against the dock below me. Mark looked up. "Get in, dork."

I froze, unsure how to react.

"Get in now or I take off without you and the deal's off. I don't care what Brian does."

"But you're supposed to watch me swim and tell Brian so I can work on the waterfront."

"It's a big lake," Mark said, sweeping his arm through the air. "You've got five seconds to get in or I'm gone, and we're done."

I clambered into the boat, standing awkwardly, causing the small boat to rock. I looked at Mark quizzically as he pushed the boat away from the dock.

"Sit the fuck down."

I froze.

Mark dug his oars into the water and pulled hard. The boat jerked forward. My knees pressed against a board and buckled. I found myself sitting on the stern thwart. Mark rowed with long pulls gliding past the boats from his rowing class.

Mark called out to the boats. "Keep rowing, guys. Remember to feather your oars after every recovery. It's the most important movement to master. If there's a wave or swell, it can pull the oar from your hands if you don't feather. If you get it right, your oar will cut right through the wave. Try it, then switch off."

Most of the scouts moved their oars awkwardly, struggling to keep them in the oarlocks, but some boats made progress rowing out into the lake.

Mark turned his attention to me, accessing my skinny, pale body and shaggy, light brown hair. "You've got balls showing up here after that psycho stunt you pulled last night."

I stared at him without replying.

"How in the hell did I get stuck with you?" Mark drawled in sync with the pull of his oars.

"Yeah. Well, I'm stuck with you too. Because of you, I've got double duty working in the kitchen and reporting to you every afternoon. You're supposed to make sure I complete the mile swim, or you go home, and I'll probably never work here again."

"So, this is all on me? All I did was push you in. Everybody treats me like I'm a criminal. Now I'm stuck with you. You're ruining my summer. It's a fuckin conspiracy."

I looked at Mark with sorry eyes. "Are you a criminal?"

"No, and don't you ever say that or I'll."

"Why did Brian call you a juvenile delinquent?"

"Shut up. You don't know me. If you know what's good for you, you'll keep it that way," Mark said with a sour look.

I didn't want to look at him, so I stared at the water and the trees along the shoreline while Mark silently pulled the oars, again and again, rowing across the lake, far from his students.

"I know you can swim," Mark said finally. "Eric said you swam to shore, so I don't know what your problem is," Mark said, lifting the oars out of the water, resting the handles in his lap.

I didn't speak.

"How hard are you going to make this for me? Can you swim or not?"

"I swim a little."

"OK, jump in."

I panicked. "Out here? In the middle of the lake."

"Sure."

"No, no… I can't."

"You swam before. Swim now."

"No. Forget it. Take me back. I'll tell Brian it's my fault." I said, trembling.

"Jump in or I'll throw you in and row back to shore without you."

I scooted back on the wooden seat, curling up next to the transom.

"I saw you that day. You were peeing yourself. Are you going to pee now? If you do, I'll make you clean the boat."

"No," I said with a whimper.

"If the guys saw you pissing yourself, you would never have lived it down. I did you a favor. They would have teased you all summer. That's why I pushed you in."

"Thanks. Sorry I ruined your life."

"People ruined my life long before you showed up. What's got you spooked? If you can swim, you can swim. It's the same water here as at the shore… just deeper."

I looked down sheepishly. "The giant sturgeons and electric eels. The sturgeon will bite me, and the eels will shock me."

"You fell for that? That's one of the oldest, lamest campfire stories of Camp Baker. What a dumb shit. There aren't any giant sturgeon or electric eels in this lake."

"But Dennis said."

"Dennis is a jackass. You're stupid if you believe him. Stand up on the thwart," Mark commanded.

"Why?"

"I want to make sure you're not peeing yourself."

"I'm not."

"Stand up."

Slowly, I stood on the wooden seat at the rear of the rowboat. "See, I'm not peeing."

Mark dug his oars into the water, pulling hard.

"No. Wait," I shouted in a startled howl, stumbling back over the transom, splashing into the lake.

The cool water was a shock. I surfaced and shook the water from my hair. "You jerk. You're an asshole. I would have jumped in if you gave me a chance. I hate you."

"Scream all you want. Nobody can hear you. Don't you know you're not supposed to stand in a boat? I can't believe you fell for that. You're so gullible."

"I hate you."

"Cool it, kid. There's no electric eels. Chill out."

I calmed as I treaded water. "And no giant sturgeons?"

"Well, no giant ones," Mark said with a smile.

"What?" I shrieked and swam for the boat.

"Siltcoos is one of the few coastal lakes in the U.S. that has sturgeon," Mark said, rowing just fast enough that I couldn't reach the boat.

"It does?" I whelped, looking into the dark water.

"They don't bite skinny white boys. Sturgeon are ugly as fuck, but harmless. The lake isn't deep, but they stay at the bottom. The sturgeon won't bother you."

I relaxed, breast stroking behind the boat as Mark rowed.

"It's the blood-sucking leeches you need to worry about. Especially if one gets stuck inside the front of your shorts."

I squealed and swam as fast as I could for the boat.

Mark laughed. "Wow, kid. You sure are dumb. Spending time with you will be a real pain in the ass." Mark leaned into his stroke and the boat pulled away from me.

"Wait. Where are you going?"

"I'm rowing. You're swimming. Swim to the shore," Mark said, jerking his head toward the beach.

I looked fearfully to the distant shore. "That's far. You're an asshole."

"I'm an asshole with a rowboat. Swim."

Mark rowed, and I had no choice but to swim. I swam with my head out of the water, afraid to put my face in the dark green murk, stopping often to rest, gasping for breath. Mark sat high and dry, yelling at me. "Keep your head down. Less splash, more go."

I swam, but it wasn't pretty. My heart pounded from the effort. I stopped often to catch my breath. My arms ached, but I kept swimming because I wanted to get out of the lake and away from that mean bastard as fast as I could.

I swam until my hand struck the hard clay of the sloping shoreline. I exited the water, panting and gasping. Mark rowed to the dock, but I didn't look back. I ran from the waterfront up the trail to the dining hall.

Just before we started serving dinner that night, Brian walked into the kitchen carrying a pair of red trunks and a white t-shirt. "Mark said you earned these today. Molly talked to me. I'm glad you fellas are working things out."

"We haven't worked out anything. Marks's a jerk. He told you I can swim?"

"He said you passed the swim test."

Even though I wanted the shorts and shirt more than anything, I hesitated. "Now you know I can swim. Do I still have to work with Mark?"

Brian winked. "The deal hasn't changed." He handed the shorts and shirt to me. "Report to the waterfront every afternoon. Mark is your coach for the mile swim. Dennis and Rusty will teach you to lifeguard. You might even have fun. Just don't—."

"I know... don't do jack shit."

Brian patted me on the shoulder and smiled. "Somebody was paying attention. See you on the waterfront, kid."

The rest of that night, all I could think about were the red shorts and white t-shirt. To me, they represented a great achievement, an earned sign of respect. The waterfront crew were the coolest guys at camp. Now that I was one of them, I could walk across the docks with my head held high, knowing I belonged. The realization that I still had to work with Mark filled me with dread.

Chapter Ten

The next morning, I wore my red shorts and white t-shirt to the kitchen. I knew I'd take some ribbing from Eric and the guys, but I was proud to wear the waterfront uniform and willing to take some abuse for the chance to show everyone I was part of the waterfront crew.

Tony looked me over. "Wow, you're finally official. No more sunbathing on the beach for you."

Eric scoffed. "Yeah, it's dress up day. Sorry, I left my clown suit at home."

James nodded at Bruce. "Every day is dress up day for Bruce."

Bruce looked down at his t-shirt. "It's Iron Butterfly day," then started singing, moving, and grooving. "In-a-gadda-da-vida, honey, don't you know that I love you? In a gadda da vida, baby."

"I've heard that on the radio," I said.

Kurt stood next to me. His scraggly sideburns had grown thicker and crawled down his cheeks to his jawline. I got the feeling that he wanted to join the conversation, but he just stood watching. Maybe he was too shy, like when I was afraid to join Brenda's group of friends. At least he never teased me.

After serving breakfast to the scouts, we ate in the dining hall at the table closest to the kitchen. I'd loaded my plate with a pile of scrambled eggs, six sausage links, and a stack of pancakes I'd cooked. That summer, I was always hungry.

I was pretty good at making pancakes. We mostly served and cleaned, but working in a kitchen, you did a little of everything. I'd ladle out two dozen puddles of batter on the five-foot-wide griddle. By the time I finished my pours, bubbles in the first cakes were bursting, signaling it was time to flip. Working my way along the griddle, I flipped them all at the perfect moment, watching the batter rise, the cakes browned and fluffy, smelling glutinously rich and hearty, then I'd scoop them up, stack them in a deep stainless pan and pour another batch.

I dug into my scrambled eggs and sausages first to make room for the pancakes. I hated it when syrup got mixed with the eggs, so I ate my pancakes last.

Tony smothered his eggs with ketchup. "I watched Mark, and you row out far from shore. Did he make you swim all the way back?"

"The jerk made me swim a lot more than a hundred yards."

Eric reached over, poked his fork in one of my sausages, and plucked it off my plate. "I heard Mark pushed you off the boat, almost drowned you."

"It wasn't like that. He's an asshole, but I didn't drown. Mark was yelling the whole time I swam. I didn't know I'd passed the swim test till Brian brought the shirt and shorts."

"It's about time," James said.

"Brian's still forcing me to train with Mark for the mile swim."

Bruce gulped down a carton of milk. "You could've avoided this whole mess if you'd done a belly flop." Bruce smiled with a look of satisfaction.

"I like working on the waterfront. It's fun," said Tony.

"It's fun for you," I said pouring an ample dose of syrup over my pancakes. "You don't have to face Mark. He's still mad, says I ruined his summer."

Eric held his fork up to his mouth, nibbling on my sausage. "I stay away from him when I work on the waterfront. I told you he's bad news."

"Honestly, Mark is scary," said Tony.

James wiped egg yolk off his plate with a piece of toast. "He stares at you like he could kill you at any moment. Criminals are like that," James said.

"The killer stare. Spooky," Bruce said with an eerie laugh.

I cut my fork through the stack of pancakes. "He told me to never call him a criminal."

Tony looked worried. "Or he'd kill you?"

Eric sat suddenly erect, like he'd had a brilliant idea. "Talk about getting murdered. Let's check out the haunted house this afternoon."

"The murdering double-bitted axe man's house?" James asked in a spooky voice.

I'd heard the campfire story about the double-bitted axe man and the mysterious house at the end of the peninsula, an area closed to campers. "Don't get murdered."

"Mark won't be with us, so we don't have to worry about getting killed. Can't say the same for you, Novak," Eric warned.

"It's just a story told around the campfire to scare young boys," Tony said.

I looked Eric in the eye. "No one's allowed down there."

"That's why we're going, idiot," said James.

"Too bad you're missing out on all the fun, Danny," said Bruce.

"Taking the chance of getting your head chopped off doesn't sound like fun," I said.

"You're working the waterfront with Mark. You're the one who should be scared," said James.

The guys would chase the legend of a murdering axeman for the pleasure of being frightened. I advanced toward fear, hoping to conquer it.

Later that day, after lunch cleanup, I changed out of my shoes, and I slipped my feet into thongs. That's what we called flip-flops, or sandals, in those days. The ones with spongy foam soles and rubber toe straps. By the time I walked out of the dining hall, the guys had already run down the main trail headed for the double-bitted axe man's house.

I paused on the trail leading to the waterfront, studying how it sloped down to the lake. From where I stood, I could spot a small patch of the blue-green water glistening in the bright summer sun. A light breeze came up from the lake carrying with it the faint sound of boys having fun, prompting me to move.

I tread slowly, allowing the descent of the trail to pull me down the hill. Stepping from craggy root to scraggly root, I walked haltingly in deep thought. Passing the swim test and working on the waterfront was my goal. Now that I had earned the red shorts, I was uneasy about seeing

Mark again. He'd made his feelings clear. I'd ruined his summer, and he hated me for it. How would he treat me now? Did he still hate me?

Step by grudging step, gravity pulled me down the hill, forcing me to quicken my pace until I stepped out of the forest, into the sun, onto the sandy beach.

I felt the warmth of the sun bake my body as I walked lazily toward the dock. Sailboats, canoes, and rowboats drifted on the rippling water.

Dennis was teaching breaststroke to a group of scouts. "What you really need to worry about are the blood-sucking leeches. They latch onto your skin with sharp teeth and suck your blood."

As usual, he was trying to scare the boys. I figured playing along was the best way to show Dennis I was on to his game, so I paused, turned my back to the docks, pulled a sock out of my backpack, rolled it up, and stuffed it in my shorts.

I then walked across the docks to Dennis. "Thank God, you warned them about the leeches. Does it look like my swelling went down?" I asked, pointing at the giant bulge in the front of my shorts.

Dennis jumped back. "Sweet Jesus."

I turned to make sure the boys in the water saw my giant swollen balls. Horrified gasps echoed across the lake.

"Is it still bad?" I asked in a panicked voice.

Dennis looked at me with a twinkle in his eye. "Oh. Yeah, it's much better now. Good thing we removed that leech before it sucked your balls off."

"Thanks, Dennis," I said, cupping my crotch. I shuffled down the dock as Dennis shouted at the boys. "No, no. Stop. Stay in the water. You guys are safe. Leech season is pretty much over."

The cowling of the speedboat's outboard motor was off, exposing the engine. Brian stood, wiping his greasy hands on a towel while Tim worked with a wrench.

I walked to the end of the dock, where Mark was teaching a canoeing class. He sat on the edge of the dock with one leg dangling in the water. A group of boys stood in a semi-circle leaning over him, watching his paddle move deftly through the water.

"This is a J stroke. Reach forward and dip the paddle in the water. Pull straight back, then toward the end of your stroke, push the paddle away from the canoe, making a J shape in the water. The J stroke allows you to paddle on one side of the canoe and move straight. The J motion leads to the recovery. Be sure to feather the paddle, reach forward and begin the next stroke." Mark looked up at the boys surrounding him to see if they understood.

"OK. Use your paddles, spread out, and try it while standing on the dock. Once you have the idea, we'll get in the canoes." Mark watched the boys move their paddles awkwardly through the air.

Mark saw me watching, observing from a distance. He stepped to me slowly as if sizing up an opponent before a fight. He glowered at me with an intense, ominous gaze trying to intimidate me, hoping I'd turn tail and run. I could have peed myself again at that moment, but I smiled.

"You again?" Mark asked.

I faced him without answering. "The way you ran off yesterday, I thought I'd seen the last of you."

Mark scared me, but I wouldn't give him the pleasure of knowing it. I reminded myself to present the confident Danny, not a frightened little boy. "You thought I was upset? Nah, I was late for kitchen duty, that's all. I'm back because this is where I want to be."

"Nice shorts."

"Brian gave 'em to me last night. Guess you told him I can swim."

"Look. I don't hate you, but I'm not your friend. You're just a skinny ass runt that Brian is forcing me to train. If I don't cooperate, he'll send me home, which is the last place I want to be. It's not personal."

I stood watching silently as Mark instructed the boys to get in their canoes. He untied a canoe, hopped in, and paddled expertly so that the canoe glided to a stop parallel to the dock in front of me. "Grab a paddle and get in."

I did as Mark instructed. I stepped to the center of the canoe, then sat on the bow seat facing forward. At least I didn't have to look at him. Mark paddled to the middle of the lake, far from the jumble of canoes from his class.

The canoe slowed, gliding silently on the water. I turned around on the bow seat to face him. "Why don't you want to go home?" I asked.

"Not your business."

"Sorry. Just wondered, since you looked scared at the thought of being sent home."

"I am not scared. Do you always ask questions that are none of your business?"

"Sometimes. Just curious since you mentioned it."

"Home is not a good option for me. I'd rather be out on the lake."

"I love camp. My family sucks, but I wouldn't mind sleeping in my own bed. Why isn't home a good option?"

"You're a fucking nosy pest, aren't you?"

"I'm just trying to make conversation."

"To quote my social worker, my home does not provide a wholesome environment. I got lucky and get to stay here."

"Why?" I asked.

Mark paddled out much farther than the previous day. "How many times do I have to tell you it's none of your business? Shut up and stop asking questions. If you repeat any of this to anyone, I will beat the shit out of you, and don't get the idea that you can hang out with me."

"OK," I said, then whispered, "Asshole."

"Get in and swim," Mark commanded.

I looked to the distant shore. "Here? This far out?"

"Why not? It's just water. I'll paddle beside you. I know you can swim, even though your form sucks. You need mileage to build endurance."

I knew that if I didn't jump in willingly, he'd toss me in or tip the canoe over to get me in the water, so I kicked off my thongs, pulled off my t-shirt and after a moment of hesitation, jumped in, causing the canoe to rock. I treaded water, leering at Mark.

"Swim with your face in the water. Nothing's gonna bite you. Every few strokes, look up and spot a point on the shoreline to target. It will help you swim straight. Now swim."

Mark had paddled out twice as far as the day before. I didn't know what he was trying to prove. I need mileage. Endurance, he'd said. Was he preparing me for the mile swim or trying to make me quit? All I knew was that I didn't have a choice, so I swam.

After a few strokes, I put my face in the water and started turning my head to breathe. My hands clawed at the water, pulling my body through the heavy liquid as Mark barked instructions from the canoe. Soon I was out of breath, but he yelled at me to keep swimming.

Earning the red shorts and t-shirt, working on the waterfront was what I had wanted, but I didn't know it was going to be like this. At that moment, I wished I'd belly flopped like Bruce. I treaded water until my heart stopped pounding, then I put my head down and swam again until I needed to rest. Stroke by stroke, kick by kick, I swam till I made it to shore.

Chapter Eleven

The staff members, a mix of college kids, high school aged scouts, and one thirteen-year-old huddled near the fireplace as a throng of scouts ran into the dining hall scurrying to their tables. Brian stood behind Mark. I stepped through the crowd to stand nearby.

"Listen up for your table assignments," said Mr. Donaldson, the senior counselor dressed in a scout uniform. "Charles, table one. Mitch, you're at table two. Dave, I'm putting you at table three. Try to keep those kids under control. Remember, you are all leaders. It's important that you set an example for the younger scouts."

Brian elbowed Mark in the ribs. "That goes double for you hot shot. Set a good example. It's part of being a leader instead of a suspect." Mark sneered at Brian.

As Mr. Donaldson continued with the table assignments, Brian noticed me standing nearby. "How's the swimming Danny? Mark hasn't drowned you yet?"

I inched closer to Brian. "Nope. We still hate each other, but he's a good swim coach."

"That's nice to hear. Let me know if there's any trouble."

I looked up at Brian, and then at Mark. "I sure will, Brian," I said with a wide smile.

Mr. Donaldson called Brian's name, and he moved to his assigned table.

Mark glared at me. "Get away from me, runt."

"I just helped you with Brian."

71

"I don't need your help. What are you doing here, anyway? Don't you work as a grunt in the kitchen?"

"I worked breakfast and lunch, so I get dinner off."

"You'd never catch me cleaning the kitchen."

"I don't mind it. Scrubbing pots is better than the chores I have at home."

Mark heard his name called. "Look who's complaining about home life now," he said, then walked to his assigned table.

I wanted to see if the guys made it back from the double-bitted axe man's house, so I slipped away to the kitchen while Mr. Donaldson raised his hands and thundered. "Quiet boys. Quiet now. No one eats until we have quiet." The room grew silent except for a few whispers and giggles. "Announcements. There will be a hike at the Oregon Dunes tomorrow afternoon. We start at the trading post directly after lunch and will return from the dunes by five p.m. Sign up with me tonight after dinner. Remember, you must get your merit badges signed off by a staff member no later than Friday afternoon. There will be an awards ceremony at the Campfire Friday night. That's it for now."

When I pushed through the swinging door, the boys were working, preparing to serve dinner.

"You guys didn't get killed by the axeman?"

Tony set a pan of thinly sliced pork chops in the warming table at the serving window. "Nope. We made it back alive, barely."

"Barely, what happened? Did you make it to the house?"

Eric juggled two large metal serving spoons, flipping one in the air, then the other, catching and tossing spoons like a circus act. "We found the house, but it's difficult to get there. You hike to the end of the trail, then push through a wall of dense brush—."

"We climbed over a fence," Bruce added, interrupting Eric.

"The no trespassing fence?" I asked.

"Yeah, that one," Eric said.

James drained a pot of veggies into a colander. "Then we crawled through a tangle of bushes, breaking branches to make a path."

"We finally we spotted the house at the far edge of a dark clearing," Tony said.

Bruce flicked his hair to get his bangs out of his eyes. "A dark and spooky clearing."

Eric spanked Bruce's ass with a spoon. "Is that why you were too scared to go any further?"

Tony carried another silver pan, this one full of mashed potatoes. "James and Bruce were so scared, they jumped at every little sound and stayed hidden in the trees."

"So did you guys, until Kurt went crazy," said James.

"We were cautious, not scared," said Bruce.

"Yeah, right," said Tony.

"It was already scary, then Kurt went on a rampage, and the fright level went off the hook," said Eric.

I looked at Kurt. He was silent as usual. Then I looked at Eric. "Kurt went on a rampage?"

Eric held up a spoon like an exclamation point. "We huddled together staring at the house, which looks remarkably like a normal shabby old place, then Kurt suddenly started marching across the clearing and up the steps of the murder house like he was ready to offer his head to the axeman."

I looked at Kurt. "Whoa Kurt." He lifted his chin with pride.

Tony jumped in. "He stepped across the porch, then just before he reached the front door, his foot went through the rotten wood."

"Up to my knee," Kurt whispered.

"Up to his knee." Eric said excitedly.

Bruce grabbed the colander and shook the last drips of water out. "It looked like the axe man was hiding under the porch, pulling Kurt down into his dungeon."

"Kurt screamed. That's when James and Bruce ran away," said Eric.

James stood in his own defense. "We retreated to a safe distance."

"Sure, you did," said Tony.

James held a steel pan while Bruce poured vegetables from the colander. "It's the smart move when facing a potential murdering monster event. Somebody has to live to tell the tale."

Tony took a spoon from Eric and pushed it into the mashed potatoes. "Kurt screamed like the axeman was about to chop his head off."

Eric grabbed his crotch. "That shriek nearly made me piss myself."

I was loving their story and wished I could have been part of their scare event. Missing out on the adventure made me wish even more that I didn't have to swim with Mark. "Did the axeman come out swinging?"

Tony wore a look of disappointment. "Nobody was home. Eric and I ran to the house and helped Kurt pull his leg out."

"You OK Kurt?" I asked.

Kurt pulled up his pant leg, displaying red scrapes on his shin and calf.

"He's fine, but that was the end of our adventure," said Tony.

"I guess you're lucky. You didn't have Mark trying to drown you all afternoon," I said.

"What happened?" Tony asked.

"The jerk paddled out twice as far as yesterday and made me swim all the way back. He was probably hoping I'd drown or give up."

Eric stuck his other spoon in the pan of succotash, or vegetable jubilee, as mom called it. "Maybe he was hoping you'd drown so he could save you and be the hero."

"I bet he'd drown you just to keep from having to babysit you every day," said James.

James's comment hurt my feelings. My face heated with anger. "He's not babysitting me." I stood facing off with James, then staring at the rest of them, I said. "I gotta get to my table," then pushed through the swinging door.

"The truth is hard to take," James shouted as I walked away.

Walking to my troop's table, I had my own scare event. Mark was sitting at the table. I panicked. I felt like running back to the kitchen. The guys would tease me relentlessly if they learned I was afraid to sit at the table with Mark. Instead, I chose to be brave, act confident, and sit at my spot next to Derek at the end of the bench.

I took a deep breath and walked to the table. Mark was shocked when I sat down across from him. "What the hell's going on? I told you to quit following me."

"This is my troop's table. I get to sit with them all week. I'd like to apologize in advance. These guys can get wild. I guess it's your lucky night."

"Why don't I feel lucky?"

Mark found himself surrounded by a dozen rambunctious young scouts. Instead of reacting to the surrounding commotion, he sat stiffly, doing his best to act leader-like. Unfortunately, ignoring the boys made them try to get his attention.

Derek, a dark-haired twelve-year-old who wore glasses, sitting next to me, said. "I can count to ten while burping." He then burp counted to ten, each belch sounding something like a number.

Mark sat motionless. I did my best to mimic Mark's rigid posture and control my emotions while surrounded by a table of rowdy heathens. I was a member of the camp staff. If I wanted to be respected by the younger scouts and accepted by the other guys on staff, I must act mature like the older guys.

Sean, a young skinny boy with a mop of dark hair, announced. "Brent can do that by farting. Show him Brent."

Brent, the chubby blond boy with pale blue eyes, promptly kneeled on the bench and pointed his butt toward the next table. Brent had the unique ability to produce multiple farts at will. The rumor, verified by several boys, was that Brent had trained his butt hole to open and gasp in air like a fish out of water. This was the secret of his spontaneous, farting prowess.

Brent began rotating his hips, preparing to blast farts. The boys at the next table scooted down the bench to get out of the line of fire. Both tables became quiet and giddy with anticipation. Brent straightened, held up his index finger as if checking the wind direction, and announced, "OK. Get ready to count."

Brent reacquired his fart firing position. The boys focused on Brent's tight olive colored scout pants outlining the round shape of his buttocks. The boys counted loudly as Brent's farts puffed, squeaked, meowed, rumbled, and chirped. There was an anxious pause. Then four farts came rapid fire like shots from a tommy gun. That's nine, the boys cheered. The tenth fart oozed and burbled. "Oops, that was a wet one," Brent said as the tables yelled, "Ten."

The boys erupted in laughter while a few gagged on the fumes, and others held their noses. One boy curled up and cried out, "I'm dying from the smell," as he rolled to the floor.

Brent's farts got me laughing, especially the wet one, but when I looked across the table at Mark, he sat rigid, unmoved by the juvenile hilarity. I quickly sat erect, composing myself.

Mark looked grimly at each boy down the length of the table. As he caught each boy's eye, they stopped laughing and straightened. One pimple-faced boy at the end of the table wasn't laughing. He was bending and twisting a paper straw and had more paper straws piled on his food tray.

"Who's that?" Mark asked.

I glanced down the table. "That's Jeff. He's an engineering genius."

"You should all be more like Jeff," Mark called out to the table.

Jeff, hearing his name, looked up briefly, holding a tangle of bent and twisted white paper straws, then grabbed another straw, folded, and bent it around whatever he was building.

Mark appeared pleased with his leadership skills. The table was quiet. Unfortunately, Mark's stone-faced tactic incited new attempts to unnerve him.

Mackey, the fat redheaded boy with a freckled face scooched in next to Mark holding a milk carton and a straw

"Watch what I can do," Mackey said, pulling a plastic cup close to him. As soon as he had Mark's attention, Mackey stuck the straw up one nostril, dipped the straw in his milk carton, inhaled some milk, then squirted a white stream out his other nostril into the plastic cup. The boys, seeing this variation of Mackey's act for the first time, erupted with cheers and laughter. Some boys chanted, "Do it again. Do it again." I fought to keep myself from laughing and maintain my mature posture.

Mark barely reacted to the triumphant Mackey with milk bubbles coming out of his nose. Instead, he cautiously scanned the room, checking the table filled with adult leaders to see if anyone was concerned about the wild boys at our table.

Mark was probably worried he'd get blamed for our table of unruly boys. I wasn't worried. Anyone who saw the guys in my troop would realize their idiocy wasn't Mark's fault. I felt sorry for him. Everyone was having fun except Mark.

I borrowed Derek's eyeglasses and placed his wire-rimmed spectacles on the tip of my nose, tilted my head down, and aimed my eyes to look over the glasses like an old professor with a grim expression and stared at Mark.

Mark accepted the challenge and locked his eyes with mine, holding a deadpan stare. "Staring contest," Derek yelled.

I looked deep into Mark's dark brown eyes, wondering why he was filled with so much anger. Mark held his stare as if he'd snagged my eyes with a treble hook and wouldn't let go. I stared back, unblinking, even after I felt the whites of my eyes drying. Mark continued to hold his steady gaze, drilling his eyes into mine.

Trying to distract him, I rolled my head back and forth, taunting him with my best comical expressions while holding his stare.

Finally, Mark burst into laughter. "Stop it. You win. Stop already." The boys laughed, and Derek declared me the winner. As the boys and I laughed, Mark regained his composure and stared at me ardently.

Surrounded by the clamor of laughter and praise, I studied him, trying to understand the unspoken meaning in his wistful eyes. When I smiled innocently, Mark turned away as if I had caught a thief.

Mark scanned the table of rowdy boys. His commanding posture and piercing dark eyes grabbed the boy's attention, causing the table to become anxiously silent. Mark broke the tension when he called out. "You guys have the sickest table I've ever seen." The boys cheered and congratulated themselves.

After Mr. Donaldson had dismissed the boys, when the large room was empty and had grown silent, a scale model of the Eiffel Tower made from paper straws sat alone on our table.

Chapter Twelve

After dinner, I hung out on the dining hall porch with the guys from my troop for a while. When they headed back to Tyee camp, I spotted a group of staff members talking near the steps. Mark was with them. I wanted to join the group, but I was hesitant to approach. My desire to be one of the gang, to be accepted by them, was strong, but fear and self-doubt held me back. I'd finally mustered the courage to walk down those steps when I heard my name.

"Hey, Mark. I heard you got stuck babysitting some kid." said Jack, who runs the archery range.

"You mean Danny?" Tim asked.

"Brian came up with a new way to punish Mark," said Dennis.

"I heard the kids working on the waterfront. Now, you'll never get rid of him," one boy said.

I stepped back, ducked to the side of the stone chimney, and listened.

"What's Brian got you doing, changing his diapers?" asked Jack.

"Nah, swimming. I hate it, but—."

"That kid is ruining your summer, man," Jack interrupted Mark.

"You won't have any fun while you're stuck with that kid," someone said.

Their words stung. They hated me. They saw me as a child, a nuisance. I wanted so much to be one of them. If this is what they thought, how would I ever fit in? I felt worthless. Squeezing my body against the chimney's hard, roughhewn stonework, I tried to make myself invisible. I pressed against the jagged rock until the rough edges dug into my skin, inflicting pain to dull the agony of rejection.

When the group of staff members walked up the gravel road toward the trading post, I jumped off the side of the porch and dashed across the assembly area.

I ran through the dark tunnel of trees and down the trail to staff camp.

When I entered my cabin, Eric was lying on his bunk thumbing a Playboy magazine.

"I'm gonna stay with my troop at Tyee camp," I said, rolling up my sleeping bag.

"Can't handle the wild night life of staff camp?"

"I can't handle you jacking off every night. You make the whole cabin shake."

"You should do it more often. You need to lighten up, nimrod," Eric said.

I ran out, letting the spring-loaded wooden door whack shut behind me.

Late evening rays of sunlight cut through the tree canopy, illuminating an ocean of ferns' golden green. I ran down a narrow unused trail, quick stepping over a gauntlet of gnarled tree roots tangled together like a bed of snakes. As the sun faded, the ferns hid in the shadows. I ran until the narrow path joined a larger trail. When I came to the twine lashed wooden gate, I pulled the pinecone, heard the gong, and gained permission to enter. Running into camp, I found an empty bunk in one of the three-sided Adirondack shelters, unfurled my sleeping bag, and laid face down on the bedroll, feeling the soft cotton fabric on my face.

Derek, the dark-haired twelve-year-old who lent me his glasses for my stare off with Mark, saw me laying on the bunk. "Hey Danny, what are you doing here?"

"I thought I'd spend the night with you guys."

"Why?"

"I need a break from being on staff."

"Why?"

"Dunno. Maybe I'm homesick."

"I'd love it if I was on staff. Those guys are cool."

Under my breath I said, "Maybe I'm not as cool as them."

I looked at Derek. From all the boys in my troop, I thought he was someone I could share my feelings, my struggle to be accepted by the older boys on staff, hoping he would understand.

"Derek, did you ever want something so bad, but no matter how hard you tried, you couldn't get it?"

Derek picked his nose, then wiped his finger on his pants. "You mean like the time I went to the corner store and bought every pack of Topps baseball cards they had hoping to get Hank Aaron, Pete Rose, or Roberto Clemente and all I got was Lowell Palmer, Terry Harmon, and other cards I already had? Like that?"

"Yeah, Derek, kinda like that."

Derek had a sudden flash of inspiration. "Hey, if Spiderman fought Batman, who do you think would win?"

"I don't know."

"How about if Batman fought Superman?"

"I don't read comic books."

"Just guess. Who would win?"

"Superman?"

"Why? Tell me why Superman wins."

"I don't want to play this game, Derek. I've got more important stuff to worry about," I said and rolled away from him.

"Well, excuse me." Derek stormed off.

This time, I didn't fight the tears. I knew I was acting like a baby, feeling sorry for myself, running back to my troop, hoping to find comfort, only to learn I couldn't share feelings with an immature twelve-year-old. What was wrong with me? I didn't feel I fit in with the guys in my troop, but the guys on staff viewed me as a little kid. I just don't fit. The guys on staff pick on me and call me a runt. I'd put up with their shit. I'd earned the red shorts, but I wasn't one of them. What did I do wrong? I was friendly, acted confident. I worked hard. No matter what I do, nobody likes me.

I heard Mackey arguing. "Just use lighter fluid." I lifted my face from the damp cotton of my sleeping bag and saw Jeff, the master craftsman, kneeling at the fire pit, stacking kindling in the shape of an Indian teepee preparing to start a fire while Brent and Derek chopped wood. Jeff pulled a metal tin from his pocket, then removed a piece of flint and a steel rod. He bent down, eyeing a clump of dried moss tucked under the teepee of tinder.

Mackey stood in front of the firepit holding a can of lighter fluid. "I'm ready when that doesn't work."

Jeff shifted the brim of his cap so it wouldn't block his view as he bent close to the dry gray-green moss. He struck the flint with the steel rod, sending sparks into the moss to no effect. Holding the flint tightly, he struck it with the steel again. This time the sparks burned the moss, creating an orange glow and a whisper of smoke. Jeff blew softly to encourage the embers to spread, but the orange glow turned black. Mackey stepped closer with his fuel. Jeff raised a hand, signaling Mackey to wait.

Sean, the skinny boy with the mop of black hair, was the lookout. His job was to watch for raiders from the adjoining camps. He sat next to a pile of pinecones the boys had gathered in anticipation of an attack. The lookout job was boring, so Sean occupied himself whittling a piece of wood. He stopped whittling when he heard sounds from the fire road that ran along the lake's shoreline below the camp. Sean scrambled to the edge of his bunker, looking down the hill at the road below. When he spotted four boys approaching in the distance, he called to the others, "Raiding party. Battle stations. Battle stations."

Jeff sent another spark into the loose ball of dried moss and this time the orange glowing embers turned red. Jeff blew lightly, and the moss ignited with a flicker of flame. He fanned the flame with his hand and blew softly. More flames appeared. When he heard Sean's battle cry, he grabbed an aluminum pot filled with a dozen arrows and sprang to action.

The boys of Tyee camp scrambled to their battle stations. Jeff had planned for an attack from the road. He and the boys had prepared artillery positions, with pinecones as their preferred weapon. They held the high ground, enabling them to rain hellfire down on that old fire road.

When Jeff moved away from the fire to prepare for battle, Mackey squirted a long stream of lighter fluid on the diminishing flames, causing the fire to roar three feet high. "Now, that's what I call a fire." Mackey tossed two logs on the blaze before taking his station.

Mark, Dennis, Tim, and Rusty snacked on candy bars and sipped soda purchased at the trading post. They walked casually on the old road, talking and laughing on their way to the waterfront.

Jeff moved from crossbow to crossbow, locking his handmade arrows into cocked positions. He had placed six crossbows along the ridgeline, aimed at the road. Derek ran stealthily on the trail toward the next camp, then carefully shuffled down the hill, and ducked behind a thicket of shrubs that hid him from the road ahead of Mark and his friends. He pulled a length of twine across the road until it was taut, secured it, then scurried back up the hill.

Brent ran out of camp, ducking under the entry gate before making his way down the hill to secure a second trip wire. When Derek returned to camp, he saw me curled on my sleeping bag.

"Come on Danny. Get up. Get to battle stations. We're being attacked." I didn't want to play war, but Derek pulled me off the bunk and led me to an artillery emplacement. A fallen log overlooking the road and a pile of pinecones, each one the size of a grenade.

Down on the fire road, Rusty's foot got snagged in the twine stretched across the road, triggering the first trip wire. One side of a tarpaulin hanging high in the trees dropped, releasing a torrent of pinecones raining down on the heads of the four boys. Startled by the onslaught, the boys ran up the road, putting them within range of Tyee camp's artillery.

The boys in camp waged a fierce attack, throwing salvo after salvo of pinecones at the confused boys on the road. Several cones hit their mark, causing Tim and Rusty to yelp and cry out. Mark and Dennis retaliated, grabbing pinecones off the road, throwing them up the hill at unseen attackers.

It became full scale war when Jeff yanked a piece of twine, sending a volley of arrows flying. One arrow hit Dennis in the butt. "Hey, that hurt," he howled. The group on the road ran from the arrows into another flurry of pinecones thrown from above.

I looked along the ridge at the other artillery positions, watching my friends work together, some throwing pinecones fending off the attackers, while other boys ran from position-to-position, resupplying ammo piles. It was a rare sight to see the boys working together. Usually, they wasted their time arguing about the simplest task, but today they worked efficiently as a team.

Jeff reloaded his crossbows and adjusted the aim. He then stood holding his twine, watching over the battle like a general waiting for the perfect moment to strike. The boys of Tyee camp were having the time of their lives, making war, relishing the heat of battle.

I'd been lobbing pinecones with little effort and no effect, but as Mark and the guys got closer, my anger swelled. They had hurt me. Now I had the chance to hurt them back. My attack became savage. I threw harder, aiming directly at Mark and the others, throwing again and again, trying my best to inflict pain.

Rusty, Tim, Dennis, and Mark threw as many pinecones as they could, but realized their counterattack was futile as more pinecones and a second volley of arrows whizzed through the air.

An arrow hit Mark on the hip, causing him to flinch. I stood, took careful aim, and threw a cone, hitting him in the head. "Yes." I yelled victoriously. Mark looked up as if he recognized a familiar voice. I ducked behind my log to hide.

Mark and the boys threw pinecones up the hill as they advanced on the road until they were out of range of our attack, but in doing so triggered the second trip wire, pulling a wedge of wood from underneath a large boulder.

Feeling safe, the boys slowed their place. "What the hell was that?" Tim asked. The heavy rock inched forward, pressing thick mud out from beneath it.

"They think we're a band of marauders." Dennis exclaimed. Branches cracked, crushed under the weight of the great stone as the boulder gained speed rolling down the steep embankment.

Mark turned toward the sound. The boys looked uphill to see a six-foot-wide boulder bounding down the hill, headed directly for them. They tried to scramble out of the way as the huge rock bounced over a tree root and crashed onto the road.

Rusty dove out of the rock's path to avoid getting squashed. The other boys pushed each other and jumped to evade the boulder as it thundered across the road and splashed into the lake. Rusty picked himself up, dusting himself off. Mark, Tim, and Dennis took a few steps up the road seeking safety. Rusty called up the hill. "That boulder could have killed me, you assholes."

"There's nothing like a good ole pinecone fight, but that rock was scary," said Mark.

"Scary? That boulder nearly crushed me," cried Rusty.

Tim surveyed the bluff. "I think I hit some of those guys."

Dennis rubbed his butt cheek. "They shot arrows at us. Real fucking arrows."

"Dennis' ass will be sore for a week," Rusty said, laughing.

"They could've put my eye out," Dennis cried.

"Yeah, if your eye was in your ass," said Tim.

"Could've been worse if the arrow hit you in the balls," said Mark.

"If Dennis had any balls," said Rusty.

The boys of Tyee camp cheered their victory. Derek and I gave each other a high-five, and everyone surrounded Jeff in celebration.

I felt invigorated. We had triumphed over the waterfront crew who hated me, but my feelings of victory quickly faded. It wasn't their words; learning how they felt about me was what hurt. I might have fought them and tried to hurt them, but I didn't hate them.

I wore the red shorts now. I still ached to be one of them, to be accepted by them. How would I face those guys the next day, knowing they thought I was a little kid who needed babysitting? My bad mood returned, covering me in a thick blanket of gloom.

Brent laid fresh logs on the fire and Mackey sprayed lighter fluid again, creating a burst of flames that shot five feet high, sending the boys reeling from the fire pit. Once the flames receded, the boys of Tyee camp gathered round the fire, telling battle stories. I sat apart from them, brooding. After a while, Mr. Hollman sat down and began telling Camp Baker's favorite campfire story; The legend of the double-bitted axe man.

Chapter Thirteen

I worked the breakfast shift. After everything was clean and put away, I walked back to Tyee Camp. My troops' visit to Camp Baker was almost over. The boys would receive their merit badges at the campfire that night, then pack up and leave the next morning. Another group of scouts would arrive on Sunday.

No one answered the gong, so I ducked under the gate. The camp was empty. My friends were in classes working on merit badges, at the archery range, the pioneering area, or a dozen other places around camp.

I went to my bunk, stripped off my clothes, and slid into my sleeping bag. I laid on my back, staring at the names and markings carved into the wooden bunk by scouts who had laid there before me. Johnny was here. Steve W. '65. K. Grimes '68. Camp Baker sucks. Carlos E.P.S. '72. I thought about all the boys who had slept in that bunk before me. Where were they now?

Someone kicked the bunk. I looked up and saw Mark standing there.

"You're supposed to request permission to enter," I said, peering out from my sleeping bag.

"You're supposed to be swimming."

"I'm not swimming, and you don't have permission to be here."

"You think I'd hunt you down and drag your ass to the waterfront if I didn't have to? The mile swim is in four weeks. If you don't swim, Brian will have my ass."

"You can tell Brian to shove it. I'm not doing the swim."

"What's your problem? First you stalk me like a freak, now you're being a punk."

"I heard you and your friends talking. You all hate me. Don't worry. I hate you too."

"Jack didn't let me finish. I was going to say I hate it, but the kid's not so bad."

"Yeah right. You say that now. Why should I waste my summer with someone who's mean and is no fun to be around?"

"Get over it. I'm mean to everybody. People have a poor opinion of me, even if they've never met me. Being mean keeps people away. Saves time."

"James and Bruce are scared of you."

"Good. Two more punks I don't need to worry about."

"If I have to waste my summer swimming, I'd rather do it with a friend."

"Don't get your hopes up, kid. Being friends with me doesn't end well."

"It's sucked so far."

Mark gave me a severe look. "You don't want me as a friend."

"Yeah, you're probably right. Go away."

"I would, but you need me to make you a swimmer."

"No, you need me to swim."

"Look, I don't like it any more than you, but we're stuck with each other," said Mark.

"If you stop being a jerk, I'll swim."

"I'll coach you if you quit being a punk."

"Can we have some fun sometimes?"

"It'll be fun if you do what I say. Now get your ass outta bed, runt. The lake is waiting,"

I figured this was as good as it was going to get. I threw my sleeping bag open, revealing my tight white briefs, climbed out of the bunk, dropped my shorts, and pulled on my red swim trunks. Mark walked on the trail out of camp while I slipped on my thongs and hurried after him.

That morning I swam like Mark's slave while he rowed lazily, calling out tips to improve my stroke. I'd heard it all before. Mark told me the same things I'd learned on the swim team three years earlier. How was my swimming punishment for Mark? This wasn't fun. He was still being a jerk. I was doing all the work. All he did was yell.

Before I left for kitchen duty, Mark made me swim a series of sprints. He said they would help me build speed. It was grueling. I wasn't sure if he was trying to kill me or getting even for the pinecone fight. He'd been to the camp; he must've known it was my troop that massacred him and the other guys. I hiked up the hill for lunch duty, exhausted.

I went back to the waterfront after the lunch shift, unsure why I continued to subject myself to Mark's torture. Maybe I hoped he wouldn't be so hard on me this time.

As I approached the dock, I saw Mark arguing with a scout leader. "I can't sign off on these merit badges," Mark said, handing several small white cards to the man. Mr. Bevins was the Scoutmaster of a troop staying at camp that week. I stayed on the beach.

Mr. Bevins took a step toward Mark. "Sure, you can. I know who you are. You're used to bending the rules, especially when it means keeping your ass out of jail. Now, I need these merit badges signed off for my boys, understand?"

"Your scouts didn't even show up for the sailing class. I can't sign these," Mark stated, raising his voice.

The Scoutmaster looked around and shouted, "Does Camp Baker management know they have a criminal working here?" He then leaned into Mark. "A person with your reputation shouldn't be working around young boys. I should report you."

Mark shoved Bevins, forcing him to take two steps back. "They know who they hired. You're lying and cheating to get merit badges. I should report you. What a wonderful role model you are, Scoutmaster," Mark said, scowling.

"How dare you hit me. That's assault. Everyone saw it. This juvenile delinquent assaulted me."

Brian, hearing the commotion, hurried across the dock, stepping between Mark and Mr. Bevins. "Both of you calm down. What's going on?"

"I asked this young man to sign these merit badge cards for my scouts. He refused and hit me."

Mark growled in frustration. "He's lying. He's a cheating bastard."

"That's enough from you, Mark. Get out of here before you make things worse."

"But those boys didn't earn the merit badges. He wants me to lie. He's cheating."

"Go now Mark," Brian scowled.

Mark stomped down the dock, got in his rowboat, and rowed away.

"That boy shoved me. He should be punished."

"Why don't you give me those cards so I can sign them, and you can be on your way?"

Bevins handed the cards to Brian. Brian quickly checked the boxes and scribbled his signature on each card before handing them back. "I don't want to see you or your boys down here the rest of the week."

"Agreed. But you better keep that maniac under control. It's only a matter of time before he hurts someone."

Brian pointed to the hill. "Leave, now."

Mr. Bevins stepped off the dock and walked proudly across the sand.

Mark was supposed to coach me, but he'd rowed out to the middle of the lake. Just as well. I didn't need him. I could swim without Mark yelling at me from the rowboat. Brian said I had to swim. He never said I couldn't swim alone. I pulled my t-shirt off, walked into the lake, and swam.

The size of Siltcoos lake is deceiving. It's larger than it seems, especially when you're swimming. The lake has an irregular shoreline with arms and inlets, not to mention the islands, peninsulas, and half submerged weed beds that can make swim navigation challenging.

I swam a third of a mile to Erhart Point, almost directly across from the waterfront. Standing on a small strip of brown clay, I set my sights on Arrowhead Point, at the southern tip of the Camp Baker peninsula.

I swam through the green water thinking how childish I had been to believe in boy biting dinosaur fish and electric eels. Moving across the calm lake below the summer sun and baby blue sky, I swam, feeling content. I tried to practice what Mark had told me, bringing my hand close to my ear, stretching out as I reached forward to begin my stroke, and rotating my hips as I pulled. I swam and swam, feeling stronger and more confident, enjoying the freedom of swimming alone.

"Breathe on both sides, runt," a voice called out, startling me.

I treaded water, glaring at Mark in his rowboat. "I'm doing fine without you."

"Are you swimming to Butterfly Island?" Butterfly Island is a long, narrow strip of dirt in the middle of the lake that barely pokes above the surface.

"No, I'm swimming to Arrowhead Point."

"Well, you're almost at Butterfly Island. Arrowhead Point is over there," Mark said, pointing.

Confused, I spun around in the water to get my bearings, then cursed myself for swimming off course.

"Did you forget to swim with your head up every fourth stroke to sight your course?"

I turned toward Arrowhead Point and swam.

"It's too far now. Even if you make it to Arrowhead Point, you'd still have to swim back to the waterfront. It's too far," Mark said, pulling slowly on his oars. I kept swimming.

For several minutes, the rowboat drifted quietly behind me as I swam.

I heard a splash and stopped swimming.

"Let's race to the waterfront." Mark had stowed his oars, then tied the rope from the bow to his ankle before diving into the water.

"I'm not racing you. You'll cream me."

"Look at me, I'm pulling the rowboat and my hip is still sore from getting shot by an arrow. I wonder who did that? You might get lucky and beat me."

Mark's comment about the arrow brought a brief smile to my lips, but I replied, "I was doing fine on my own before you showed up."

"Okay, if you keep swimming the direction you're headed, you'll end up at Reed Island or drown trying to get there. Don't you know you're supposed to swim with a buddy?"

"So, you're my buddy now?"

"Swim buddy. I'd never let anything bad happen to you while you're in the water. It's my superpower."

His comment surprised me. He'd never said a nice word to me before then. "Now you're my swim buddy with superpowers. You just let me swim off course."

Mark laughed. "You didn't want my help, so I let you swim. I'll share a secret that helps me. It's my swim mantra."

"Mantra? What's a mantra?"

"It's like a meditation. Words you repeat to yourself to stay focused while you swim."

"Words you repeat, a mantra. What are they?"

Mark moved his arms and head, mimicking the swim movements as he recited his mantra. "Left, right, left, breathe right. Left, right, breathe left. Stroke left and right with head up, sight the course, head down, kick, kick. I repeat those words to myself over and over as I swim. It helps me concentrate on my stroke, and I never go off course. Try it."

I visualized the movement of my arms, turning my head to breathe and swimming with my head up to sight while I mouthed the words.

Mark tilted his head to the north. "Follow me to the docks. I'll set the pace."

Treading water, I turned to face the waterfront. It was so far away. I could barely make out the white docks in the distance. How did I get so far off course? I didn't want to show my distress, so I agreed to follow him.

Mark set a steady pace. It was exhausting, but working to keep up, I swam better.

Even though I was chasing Mark, I repeated the swim mantra to myself over and over. Running those words through my brain, I never strayed from the course, and felt my stroke become more consistent, rhythmic.

Left, right, left, breathe right. Left, right, breathe left. Stroke left and right with head up, sight the course, head down, kick, kick.

Chapter Fourteen

At the end of that second week of summer camp, my scout troop left Camp Baker. It was a hot Saturday morning when I stood in the parking lot waving at cars and pickups loaded with boys as they drove away. I felt a strange emptiness watching the dust hang in the air as the vehicles disappeared in the haze. I have never felt so alone as I did at that moment.

I told myself that everything would be all right. I would rely on myself, just as I always had. Early that morning, I had moved back to the cabin I shared with Eric. No matter what happened the rest of that summer, there would be no troop from home I could run to, hoping to find comfort and protection. No matter how bad things got, I knew there was no one who would come to my rescue.

I would navigate through the drudgery of my life, saddled with the burden of making it on my own. I had me. Suck it up and tuck your worries away. Nobody would know my struggles unless I let them show, so I hid my fears behind bright eyes and a smile. The world would see the best Danny Novak I could muster. That spunky boy without a worry or a care.

Saturday lunch was light duty. With the previous week's campers headed home, the kitchen was less frantic than usual. Mom and the assistant cooks prepared a simple lunch for the camp staff.

Tony cut tomatoes for sandwiches. "Did you guys hear about Mark getting into it with that Scoutmaster yesterday?"

"They would have thrown punches if Brian hadn't broken them up," said Eric.

I looked up from scrubbing a pan. "Mr. Bevins was cheating. The boys in his troop didn't earn those merit badges. They'd hardly been to the waterfront."

"Mark's lucky Mr. Bevins didn't press charges, or Mark would end up in prison again," said Tony.

I was confused. "I heard he was in juvie. Why would Mark end up in prison?"

Tony stopped cutting tomatoes and looked at me cockeyed. "You don't know? Everybody knows."

"People said Mark was a criminal and put in detention. I didn't know he was in prison."

James walked toward me. "The cops arrested Mark a couple of years ago for killing his uncle."

"They got him for stealing his uncle's car. He was in jail for months," Bruce added.

James spun his towel, preparing to smack it. "The murder was never solved, so they finally let him go."

I gasped with sudden awareness. "Why didn't you tell me this? I've been swimming with a killer, and you never told me."

Eric stared at me like I was an idiot. "I told you he was bad news."

I pointed at Eric, accusing him. "Bad news is a long way from a murderer." I looked at the other guys. "So, that's why you're all afraid of him."

Tony pushed his mop across the floor. "He's not exactly friendly."

Bruce put a stack of clean plates on a shelf. "He acts like he wants people to fear him."

"He said he acts mean because people have a bad opinion of him," I said.

"Yeah. People usually have poor opinions of murderers," James said.

Eric looked at me like I was a dumb shit. "You've never heard this? What rock are you living under, Novak?"

"I don't watch the news." I didn't mention that Billy broke the dial on our TV, so we only got one channel. At least I could still watch Gilligan's Island.

James laughed. "Eric thought you were brave, spending time with Mark. Now we know you're just a dipshit."

"So, who killed his uncle?" I asked.

Mom pulled a tray of baloney boats out of the oven and set them on the table. "No one knows Danny. Mark was never in prison. He was in juvenile hall. Now, that's enough gossip. I swear you boys are worse than a bunch of old ladies in a knitting circle. We know Mark was falsely accused. I can't imagine what he went through. Come on, let's get ready to serve lunch."

Saturday's were our day off. Many of the adult staff and older boys would go into town to shop, run errands, or drink beer and relax before the next group of boys arrived on Sunday. Tim, Dennis, and Rusty went to town with Brian to pick up parts for the speedboat. James and Bruce caught a ride with Jack. With no friends around to hang out with, Mark approached me after lunch.

"Wanna go canoeing?"

"No, thanks." After what I'd just learned, I had second thoughts about spending time with Mark, but the gossip did make me curious. Mom said he was falsely accused, and he hadn't killed me yet.

"Come on, it's a great day for paddling."

"If you mean me swimming and you in the canoe? No thanks, it's my day off."

"You in the canoe. No swimming. I got nothing else to do, and you need the mileage."

Mileage. It didn't matter if it was swimming, rowing, or canoeing. Mark always said I needed mileage. I was pretty sure I was the last person he wanted to spend time with. If Tim or Dennis were around, he would be with them.

The guys from the kitchen crew had scattered. Canoeing sounded better than swimming, and I wanted to learn more. I realized I knew nothing about Mark.

I paddled the canoe while Mark sat backward on the bow seat, facing me. Mark had run me through a rigorous examination, testing every stroke required to earn the canoeing merit badge. "I thought this was my day off. You turned it into a test. Did I at least pass?"

"You passed. Good thing you did. Brian expects you to teach the class next week."

"No problem. I'm in the water every day now. I'm not like that cheater, Mr. Bevins."

Mark shifted uneasily on the aluminum seat. "I hate people like him. They Judge me because they think they know something. They don't know shit."

"Did he think you'd cheat because you've been in prison?" I asked.

"Screw you. I wasn't in prison. Jesus Christ. Please let me go someplace where no one has ever heard of me. Nobody ever sees me. They only see headlines and news reports."

"I just heard the guys talking."

"You know, you were the one person. The only person who didn't judge me. Out here on the lake, whenever we spent time together, I didn't have to think about my past. I could relax and be myself. Now you bring up this shit."

"The guys were talking, I—."

"Fuck you. The perfect suburban white boy living your privileged, whitewashed life. You heard some bullshit gossip, now you judge me."

Mark's rebuke stung. "Perfect life? You know nothing about my life."

"Oh, it's rough living in the big house with two cars in the driveway. How hard could your life be, skinny white boy? What? Daddy didn't buy you the latest video game. Don't make me cry."

I clenched my teeth and squinted; my eyes zeroed in on Mark. I'd worked hard to stay positive and confident, but Mark's words stunned me. I breathed deeply. The shame I felt about my home life boiled to the surface. The façade I'd created melted away. I fought to hold back my emotions, but I couldn't help myself. Feelings I wished were buried deeper boiled to the surface.

"I live in a shit hole rented house. We're poor. My dad dumped my mom and moved away. She works at the Ford dealer and gets paid crap. She's never home; always drinking and fucking the salesmen. If she's not bringing home a man, it's a stray dog or cat. We have so many animals I lost count. My house smells like piss and shit."

"Oh damn. That sucks."

"My mom pays me fifty cents a week to scoop dog crap in the garage. Did you ever have a pool of dog piss splash you in the face?"

Mark recoiled. "No."

"Do you go to school smelling like dog shit and get teased every day? I joined the scout troop at the Catholic church on the other side of town so nobody would know me. I'm not even Catholic. You know nothing about my life." My body flushed hot with anger. I struggled to breathe as I held back tears, staring at Mark.

"That's fucked up. How would anyone know? You look like the perfect little white puke who has everything," Mark said.

"Maybe being white is a good disguise. Everybody expects your life to be perfect, but it's fucking not."

"Sorry man. Do you ever see your dad?"

"No. I usually get a card with a few bucks at Christmas, but sometimes he forgets. I heard you live with your dad."

"Only because I have to."

"You don't like him?"

Mark looked across the lake for a moment, then turned back to me with a sad face. If he could have shed a tear, he would have.

"My mother was a Latino woman. They say she was beautiful and sweet."

"That's why you have a good tan," I said in sudden realization.

"What the fuck?" Mark glared at me.

"Sorry. Keep going."

"My Dad killed her when I was four."

"Oh, shit."

"He went to prison for ten years. They sent me to live with my Uncle John."

"That's horrible."

"Life with John was great. I wish he was my dad. He took me to swim lessons and swim club. We joined the boy scouts. We went camping and hiking. I played football in middle school. I got good grades."

"It sounds like you're living the perfect white boy life."

"It was a great life."

"Was?"

"After my dad got out of prison. He and John met a few times. I don't know what they talked about, but it always ended in a fight."

"You didn't want to live with your dad?"

"I don't know him. I hadn't seen him for ten years. He got a job at a lumber mill nearby, but I didn't see him often."

"Then what happened?"

"I was fourteen. Sometimes, I would sneak out at night and drive John's car down to the river. I didn't do anything crazy. I just needed to get out and think, ya know."

"You stole his car?"

"I drove it. I always brought it back. He was asleep. I don't think he knew. Maybe he did. It doesn't matter. One night when I drove home, police cars with their flashing red and blue lights had surrounded the house."

"Someone murdered your uncle, and the police blamed you."

"The cops suspected me. They suspected my dad too, but he was working graveyard at the mill."

"Eric said it was on the news."

"It was on the news and in the papers. They made me out to be a big time criminal and murder suspect. It didn't take long for the cops to know it wasn't me, but they stuck me in juvenile detention. There was no place for me to go. It took months for the court to release me into my dad's custody."

"If you live with your dad now, why did you say your home isn't a suitable environment?"

"He doesn't know me. He's a miserable drunk with no friends. The man killed his wife, and his brother is dead. We don't get along. Sometimes it gets loud." Mark looked sad.

I sat silently, watching him.

"Neighbors called the cops a few times. My choice for the summer was camp or a foster home. I chose camp."

"What happens after the summer?"

"My counselor said I can try living with my dad again. He joined AA. Maybe separating us for a few months will make things better. If we still don't get along, I'll be in a foster home."

"Our lives are fucked up," I said in a sad tone.

"Everywhere I go, people look at me and see a criminal. As soon as I can, I'm gonna get away, go someplace where people don't know me. Sometimes it gets so bad that I think about swimming out into the ocean and never coming back. Maybe out there, deep below the sea, I'd find peace."

"When you're older, you can move to a place where nobody knows your name. I'm gonna move out as soon as I turn eighteen."

"So, you can have your own house full of dogs and cats?" Mark said, smiling.

"I'll never live with animals again."

Mark leaned back in the canoe's bow with his hands behind his head, absorbing the afternoon sun. "A criminal and a shit shoveler. What a pair."

I paddled slowly across the calm water while we basked in the summer sun and shot the shit about our crappy lives.

Chapter Fifteen

Saturday nights tended to get wild. The boys and young men living in staff camp were unsupervised, and with no scouts around, we had no responsibilities.

Kurt and Tony shared a cabin and had invited the kitchen crew to party at their place that night.

We'd never been to their cabin. Eric was excited, as usual. He was always up for a good time. "Time to get your groove on Danny boy," he said, running out of the cabin. I rushed to catch the door to keep it from slamming. I hated that sound.

We saw Mark, Tim, and Rusty enter Dennis' cabin as we walked across camp. I assumed Dennis planned another night of porn.

Tony must have heard us coming up his cabin's steps because he called out, "Take your shoes off before entering. Kurt's rule."

I kicked off my thongs. When I opened the door, I faced a beaded curtain; long red strings threaded with colored beads and bits of polished bamboo. I pushed apart the colored strings and stepped in, letting the long threads swing. The beads clicked behind me as they swung back in place. While my mind was unwrapping the weirdness of walking through a bead curtain, my feet luxuriated in the comfort of red shag carpeting covering the floor. Soft and cozy on my feet, and red as maraschino cherries. Draped across the ceiling, a Union Jack flag dimmed the cabin's light, adding to the tonal aura of the room.

This cabin didn't have bunks, just single beds on each side. There was a shelf on the far wall between the beds made from a wide board nailed to two by fours as legs. A boxy blue and white portable record player sat on the shelf next to Kurt's bed. On the right side, by Tony's bed, was a row of soda bottles dripped with candle wax from long white candles and a lava lamp glowing with green globs floating, sinking, and breaking apart. Below the makeshift shelf was a stack of records.

Tony sat on a milk carton on his side of the cabin and Kurt sat in his bed with his back against the wall. I didn't recognize the upbeat piano music coming from the phonographs speaker, but it sounded jazzy.

Posters covered the walls, as you'd expect, but there were no Playboy playmates of the month. They were all European sports cars; a BMW E3, a Porsche Targa, a Triumph Spitfire, and a Lamborghini Miura, all spaced a safe distance from a dart board placed at the center of the back wall above the shelf.

Eric pushed past me. "This place is wacko, man."

I was still taking everything in but added, "Yeah. Cool."

Tony pointed to two milk cartons for us to sit on. "It's eclectic."

Kurt stood. He wore a maroon silk robe and held a pipe in his hand. "It's sophisticated."

It still amazed me, the lengths some boys went to decorate their cabins. "You guys brought all this stuff?"

Tony raised his hand. "I brought the dartboard."

Kurt raised a Zippo lighter to his pipe, puffing vigorously. "We're here the entire summer. Why not be comfortable?"

"That's what I'm saying," said Eric.

A sweet, musky aroma of warm cherries filled the room.

"What's that music?" I asked.

Kurt removed the pipe from his mouth. "Thelonious Monk." He said the words in a tone that implied I should know that.

"Never heard of him. What else you got?" I scooted across the carpet and started flipping through the records. "You've got a great record collection."

Tony leaned toward me. "They're called LPs. Kurt gets upset if you call them records."

I flipped through LPs with names like Chick Corea, Weather Report, Lester Young, Keith Jarrett, Miles Davis, and Pat Metheny. "There's no famous bands here. What are these?"

Kurt puffed his pipe and exhaled a gray cloud. "They're legendary jazz musicians. The best of all time."

Eric looked Kurt over. "You never say much in the kitchen. I didn't know you were so snooty."

"Sophisticated," Tony corrected. "Kurt goes to a private school up by Portland where they cultured him."

"Cultured like yogurt," Eric said.

Kurt held his pipe a few inches from his mouth. "The Gables follows a European curriculum that expands the students' minds, providing them with a broad overview of culture, social science, and intellect. They expose us to much more of the world than public schools."

I looked up from the records. "I just thought you ran the dishwasher good. How did a guy like you end up here?"

"I operate the dishwasher well because it's the job I'm tasked with performing." Kurt then dropped the elite attitude. "My dad made me take the job. He said I need to be more down to Earth. You can't get more down to Earth than living in a forest and washing dishes. My mom picked the school."

"I never met a rich guy before," I said.

"We aren't rich."

Eric sat on a milk carton. "Anybody cultured as you gotta be rich."

I was curious about Kurt and his life. We worked in the same kitchen, but we were so different, and I didn't even know it until now. "Did you ever take a family vacation?"

Kurt appeared guarded as he puffed his pipe. "Do you consider summering in Italy, vacation? It's my grandfather's villa."

"Hell yeah." Eric fell off his milk carton and rolled on the cherry red carpet, laughing.

Italy. I could barely imagine it. All that came to mind was the Leaning Tower of Pisa. Or was it pizza? "We spent a weekend in Medford once," I announced.

Kurt, embarrassed, sat on his bed.

"He's an aristocrat, but he's cool once you get to know him," Tony said.

Eric climbed back on his milk carton. "It's good to know you, Kurt. You should have said something sooner."

"I didn't want to stand out."

Tony raised his hand with the scout sign. "He swore me to secrecy."

"I just want to be a regular guy. One of the fellas."

"You're one of us, man," Eric cheered.

I moved back to the stack of LPs. "You're as regular as Swiss cheese. Now, have you got any real music?"

Kurt moved off his bed and joined me on the floor. He flipped through his collection and pulled out two albums. "I have Simon and Garfunkel's Bridge over Troubled Water, or ZZ Top."

"ZZ Top. I heard of them. How do you go from felonious monk to ZZ Top?"

"It's Thelonious. I like their beards."

While Kurt was changing the record, James and Bruce appeared at the door. "Shoes off. Kurt's rule," Tony shouted.

James pushed through the bead curtain and shouted, "Let's party, boys."

Bruce then emerged through the beaded veil, brushing his hand through his heavy metal hair, wearing a Deep Purple t-shirt. "Wow, cool robe, Kurt."

"He smokes a pipe," I added.

James scanned the room. "This place rocks."

ZZ Tops, La Grange began playing.

"I love the Euro vibe of his place," Bruce said.

"Does anybody want to play darts?" Tony asked desperately.

"Look what we got." James turned to show the back of his jeans. Bruce did the same. Both boys jutted their hips, displaying bottles sticking out of their back pockets. They reached back, pulled out the bottles, and announced. "Mad Dog 20/20."

"Now it's a party. How did you get those?" Eric asked.

Bruce sat on Tony's bed. "There's a small market on the edge of town. We dared each other to go in and buy booze. James looks older, and he's taller, but he was too scared to try."

"James is a chicken," said Eric matter-of-factly.

"Screw you, Eric. I never bought booze before, have you?"

Bruce continued. "I walked in the store all casual like and went directly to the alcohol. When I set two bottles of grape Mad Dog on the counter, the old lady at the register looked me in the eye and asked;

would you like a bag for those, honey? I said sure, paid, and walked out. When I was in the clear, I ran to where James was hiding. It just takes balls, man."

Bruce and James gave each other a high five and shouted, "Mad Dog."

"What is it?" I asked.

Eric got in my face. "It's booze, hooch, firewater, liquid courage, jungle juice, vino. Haven't you drunk wine before?"

"I took a sip of beer once. It tasted like piss." I didn't add that it was a beer one of my mom's boyfriends had left on the table after they moved to her bedroom.

James looked at me curiously. "You've never been drunk?"

"Nope," I said, shaking my head.

"We can fix that," James said, sitting on a milk carton. His legs stretched across the gap between beds and extended under Kurt's bed.

Bruce held up his bottle. "Mad Dog is 20 percent alcohol in a 20-ounce bottle. Its strong grape-flavored wine. It might not taste great, but it does the trick."

"Is that enough for all of us?" Eric asked.

Kurt crawled under his bed and handed me bottles. "I have a fifth of Jack Daniels and Southern Comfort," he said.

"I have plastic cups," Tony offered.

"I've got cards. How 'bout we play a drinking game?" James suggested.

Bruce and James huddled together, whispering, then Bruce said, "OK. Let's play Hi/Lo. It's a great drinking game. I'll deal."

"How do you play?" I asked.

James moved from his milk carton down to the carpet, then turned a second carton upside down to make a table. "Hi/Lo is the simplest card game ever. That's why it's great for drinking. We take turns. When it's your turn, you bet if the next card drawn is going to be higher or lower than the last card dealt. If you guess wrong, you drink. Last man standing wins."

Everyone sat on the maraschino cherry shag, and Tony put out six plastic cups he'd borrowed from the dining hall. James cracked open the twist-off cap of his Mad Dog and poured some into each glass, then handed the deck of cards to Bruce, who shuffled like a professional dealer.

James lifted his glass. "OK, everybody has the first drink together." We clinked our plastic cups and yelled, "Cheers."

"Bottoms up," Bruce said. James and Bruce dumped the flavored wine down their throats.

I waited and watched the others. "Just guzzle it. You might not like the taste," Eric advised before drinking his down and grimacing afterward.

I downed mine and nearly died gagging. "That stuff tastes like crap."

James poured himself another portion and downed it. "The more you drink, the better it tastes."

Kurt raised his bottle of Southern Comfort. "Mad Dog is more about getting a buzz than savoring the process. Try this. It tastes better." Kurt poured the golden liquor into my cup.

Bruce cut the cards and shuffled once again. "Ready to play. I'll lay down the first card." Bruce dealt a card face up on the table. "It's a seven. James goes first.

"Happily," James said, pouring a half inch of Mad Dog into his glass. "Low."

Bruce dealt a card, laying it facing up. "Five. You guessed right, you win."

"Damn." James drank the jungle juice, anyway.

"No, no, no. You only drink if you lose," Bruce scolded.

James leaned against the bed. "Why does winning feel like losing?"

It was Eric's turn. James poured some Mad Dog into his glass. Eric studied the five of diamonds lying face up. "High."

Bruce dealt a two of hearts. "We have a loser. Drink up."

Eric brought the glass to his lips, hesitated, then gulped the purple liquid. "Blech. Yeah, I think I'm acquiring the taste of this rotgut."

Kurt poured himself a shot of Jack Daniels. "High."

Bruce threw down a nine of spades. "Kurt's a winner."

Kurt saluted Bruce. "The sober victor."

My turn was next. I thought about the nine of spades. There were more lower numbered cards than higher cards. I made the logical choice. "Lower."

Bruce threw down the Jack of clubs. "Drink up, Danny boy."

I lifted my glass and felt vapors from the liquor swirling under my nose before the liquid touched my lips. It tasted like spiced honey, orange cough medicine. I drank it down and felt a warm glow in my chest afterward. "I like this one," I said, holding my glass out for Kurt to refill.

Tony lost and Bruce won. We went several times around. James, Bruce, and Eric guzzled grape rag water, Tony and I imbibed the nectar of the gods, Southern Comfort, and Kurt tippled the spirit of Jack Daniels.

Somehow, I lost every turn, but I was feeling good. "This tastes like Christmas." I poured myself an extra portion to sip since the game had paused.

"Princess Leia is hot," Eric shouted. Star Wars had come out the previous summer and the movie was still a topic of conversation.

"Luke's gonna make it with her. Wait till the next movie," said James.

Bruce stood in protest and shouted. "It won't happen. Leia loves Han Solo." He fell onto Tony's bed, then slid back to the floor.

"Tony kinda looks like Luke Skywalker," Eric said.

Tony stood, grabbed a pop bottle with a long white candle attached and waved it around, making light saber sounds. When he kicked the milk carton table, everyone lunged for their glasses.

Eric cradled his rescued glass. "You're so fucking drunk, man. You almost spilled my vino de milo."

"I ain't drunk," Tony stumbled. "I'm Luke and I'm gonna light saber your ass," he said, swinging the candle, making light saber sounds.

Kurt puffed his pipe. "May the force be with you."

I leapt to my feet and started shouting. "I'm floating," staggering past the milk cartons. "It feels like I'm flying. I've never felt this good before. I'm perfect. Can you see me? This is the real me. Do you see me now?" I screamed.

James and Bruce held each other, giggling as I continued my drunken rant. "This is the real me. I'm a Jedi." I stood breathing hard. "The force is in me," I shouted.

Kurt noticed Bruce and James laughing at me. "What did you guys do?"

James stopped giggling long enough to explain. "We rigged it, so Danny drank every turn."

"He's wasted," Bruce added.

James laughed again. "He said he'd never been drunk before, so we helped the runt out."

The cabin door opened, and Mark threw the beads aside. Tim, Rusty, and Dennis crowded the steps behind him. "What the hell is going on? The entire camp can hear you guys."

I stepped forward, sweeping my hand broadly. "These aren't the droids you're looking for."

Mark looked concerned. "What did you guys do to him?"

"Don't worry. I'm the real me now. People like me. I have friends, not you."

Rusty pushed into the room. "He's drunk."

Mark looked mad. "Eric and Tony. You guys are waterfront. We're supposed to stick together."

"We're drunk too." Eric said, waving his glass. Tony buzz buzzed, swiping his candle stick.

Mark pointed an accusing finger. "Stop treating him like a punk. He's one of us."

"He's fine. We're just having fun," Bruce replied.

Even in my drunken stupor, I realized Mark was being protective. I felt bad saying he wasn't my friend. He'd stuck up for me. Nobody had ever done that before. I wanted to thank him, but the cabin started spinning. I held up my hands, motioning for everything to stop. "The force is spinning. Stop spinning." I stumbled.

Eric kept me from falling. "I've got a bad feeling about this," he said.

I staggered forward, feeling green. A nauseous queasiness roiled in my stomach. "I don't feel so good." I weaved past Mark and Rusty, rushing for the door. Dennis jumped off the steps as I lunged forward and heaved my guts out.

Hot frothy liquid splashed against the hard ground, spreading bronze pine needles awry. My stomach convulsed again, turning my guts inside out, and another fountain expelled out of my mouth. It hurt bad but felt so good. Afterward, I stood bent over, elbows on my knees, spitting bile, staring at the bits of digested food and grape-colored fluid mixed with damp pine needles. My stomach rejected the honey spirits once again, but there was no fountain, only the pain of a dry heave.

I was about to sit on the ground, but Dennis and Tim grabbed me by the arms and guided me to the steps. "The force is strong with this one," Tim said.

"Hell yeah, man. The force gushed out of him like a fire hydrant," said Dennis.

I curled on the steps, sucking in air, praying I wouldn't be sick again. Mark and Rusty jumped over me to the ground. "He'll be fine after he sleeps it off," said Tim.

Mark squatted down, checking on me. "He's not such a bad kid once you get to know him."

Rusty looked at Tim and Dennis. "You know, one time he helped me secure the sail boats when a bunch of kids ran off."

Tim gazed thoughtfully. "He helped me knock down the head of every rusty nail on the docks."

Dennis smiled warmly. "Did I tell you guys he scared the crap out of my swim class? He stuffed his shorts. Told the boys a leech had got him. His balls were ginormous. It was hilarious. We scared those boys shitless."

Eric appeared at the door. "Jesus, he's drunk, not dead. Stop with the fucking eulogy. The kid's still a putz, but he's alright."

The guys walked me to my cabin, and I crawled into bed.

Somehow, I woke up on time to work the breakfast shift. The resilience of youth.

Chapter Sixteen

The next week, an adult leader named Mr. Curtis brought his sailboat to camp. This sailboat was nothing like the old wooden dinghy's with faded blue hulls Camp Baker had. This sailboat was a Laser, a sleek racing sailboat. From the red low-profile fiberglass hull to the flat white deck, and the red laser beam on the sail, everything about that boat screamed fast. They designed the laser for two people, but when racing, it's a one-man boat. You sit on the wide flat deck and put your feet in a small center cockpit.

The first time I saw the Laser was when Mark went sailing with Mr. Curtis. Mr. Curtis was in control of the boat with one hand on the tiller and the other hand holding a rope called the mainsheet. The wind was blowing steady that afternoon. Once Mr. Curtis turned the boat downwind, off they went.

Later, I watched as the Laser came about and tacked across the wind. Suddenly, one side of the boat lifted out of the water. Mark and Mr. Curtis had to lean back to keep the boat from flipping over. It was beautiful. They were flying with the wind.

I was supposed to be lifeguarding, but I couldn't take my eyes off that boat. When they returned, I ran to them and helped tie the bowline to a dock cleat. I could tell they'd had a great time. Mr. Curtis and Mark looked ecstatic, wearing broad smiles and windswept hair. Excitedly, I asked Mr. Curtis, "Will you teach me to sail?" He stepped onto the dock and said, "Mark can teach you. He's an excellent sailor."

Mark removed the daggerboard, then looked at Mr. Curtis. "You mean I can take it out by myself?"

Mr. Curtis smoothed his hair. "Sure, I brought it to be sailed. You know what you're doing. Take it out whenever you like." Mr. Curtis then pointed at me. "This boy looks like he's fallen in love with my Laser. You'd better take him out with you."

Tony agreed to take over lifeguarding while Mark took me sailing. We sailed with our shirts off, absorbing the warmth of the sun mixed with the cool spray splashing us from the bow. For a while Mark sailed west to east, letting the sheet out, running with the ocean breeze filling the sail. He sat tall with his hand on the tiller. When he called, "coming about," Mark pulled the tiller toward his body and pulled in the mainsheet as the boat suddenly turned. I spotted the boom coming at my head just in time, ducking under as it swept past.

The boat had turned enough that the wind quickly filled the sail. We were now moving across the wind. "This is called tacking," Mark said. The Laser took off like a particle of light skipping across the water. As Mark pulled the sheet tighter, the side of the boat we sat on began lifting out of the water. Spray from the bow hit my face, and the wind blew through my hair. I felt pure joy sailing under the cornflower blue sky. I was alive and free as the breeze. Mark leaned back, his six-pack stomach flexing as he let his upper body go out over the edge of the boat. He leaned back so far; his long black hair dipped into the water.

"Lean back," Mark shouted. "This is called hiking out. Our weight keeps the boat from heeling over."

I leaned back, feeling the raised hull cutting through the water. I looked at Mark. "This is amazing." Mark smiled devilishly, then suddenly pushed the tiller away from his body as he sat up. The Laser slammed down hard, and I fell, tumbling into the lake. "You jerk. I'm not swimming back," I yelled, treading water.

Mark brought the Laser around and sailed to me. "Didn't I tell you about the toe strap? You're supposed to keep your feet under the strap when you're hiking out, otherwise you might fall in the water."

"I think you forgot to explain that."

Mark steered the Laser into the wind letting the sail luff while I pulled myself onto the boat. I sat and put my feet under the hiking strap. "Teach me to sail."

"All right. Switch places." I grabbed the tiller with my right hand and Mark passed me the sheet. As we sailed, he explained parts of the sailboat, taught me to tack, how to let the boat run with the wind, how to come about, and how to hike out.

Every time we caught the wind on a tack and the boat heeled up, I tried to dump Mark like he had done to me, but it never worked. He was too smart to be fooled by his own trick.

That afternoon, Mark wore a constant smile. It didn't matter if he was gliding over the water in a Laser, rowing his favorite rowboat, or swimming, Mark loved the water. He'd said he felt most comfortable in the water, and he showed it.

Once, while we were hiking out, he let his hair drag in the water again, then suddenly, he released his feet, and his body slipped away, submerging deep into the lake. I let up on the mainsheet and pushed the tiller away from my body to come about, but Mark was gone. The sail luffed in the wind as I scanned the surface. I was worried, calling out his name, watching, looking for him to come up. It felt like minutes passed before he silently surfaced behind me, spitting a fountain of cool water on my hot skin. I jumped at the shock. "You scared me. I thought something happened to you."

Mark pulled himself onto the boat. "I love the water; it sets me free. I am one with the water and the water is one with me," he said with religious reverence.

We spent that golden summer afternoon free from cares or worry sailing on the cool breeze, trying to make each other fall in the water or take the others head off coming about, racing with the wind on a laser beam. I turned fourteen that day. I didn't tell anyone, not even Mark. Being on the water sailing the Laser till dusk was the best birthday gift I could have wished for.

One night after dinner, I went to the trading post to buy an Almond Joy candy bar. I enjoyed the creamy coconut, letting the chocolate melt in my mouth, swirling the coconut over my tongue, then crunching down on the almond. I liked the jingle too. Sometimes you feel like a nut, sometimes you don't. It was nearly impossible to eat an Almond Joy and not have that song play in your head as you munched on the almond.

I walked north through knee high shrubs on lightly traveled trails exploring a part of camp I rarely visited when I heard someone chopping wood. I walked through the woods, following the sound, until I came to a clearing and saw Mark swinging an axe behind the caretaker's house.

He placed a large piece of wood on a stump and split it in half with a single swing of the axe; the pieces falling to the ground. He put one half back on the stump and split it again, and did the same to the other piece, then picked up the split wood and laid it on a long pile of chopped wood.

"What are you doing?" I asked when I got close.

"Chopping wood. What does it look like?"

"I thought you only worked the waterfront."

"I'm helping Mr. Farnsworth. He needs wood for the camps and the dining hall fireplace."

"Why?"

"Because he asked me. He's about the only adult around here that gets me. We talk sometimes and we help each other out."

I'd seen Mr. Farnsworth around the camp. He drove a small garden tractor with a trailer to haul firewood, and I'd seen him doing maintenance on the buildings. To me, Farnsworth looked like a farmer because he always wore blue overalls and a worn baseball cap. The old fella seemed friendly enough, but I'd never talked with him. I'd heard that he'd lost a son a few years earlier, in the Vietnam war. Maybe having Mark around helped him deal with his loss.

"Need help?" I asked.

Mark swung the axe. "Nope."

"You going to hang out at Dennis's cabin later?"

"Nope." He split a log in half.

"See you tomorrow?"

"Sure."

I got the feeling Mark didn't want company, so I left him to his wood chopping.

The rest of the week swept by fast. Another group of scouts came and went. You learned some names and remembered a few faces, but it was impossible to know them all. New boys would soon replace the boys from this week. And there would be hundreds more scouts the week after that.

I spent every free moment I had on the waterfront. I swam, but also worked as a lifeguard, sailed, and rowed.

Before I knew it, another Saturday had come. The scouts we'd taught departed with new skills, merit badges earned, and stories they would share for a lifetime.

After lunch cleanup, I ran out of the dining hall and down to the waterfront. As I ran across the sun scorched dock, Mark, Rusty, and Tim were paddling away in canoes. I stood hesitantly at the edge of the dock watching them drift away, longing for the older boys to include me. I was about to turn and walk back to camp when I heard Mark.

"Hey Danny," He called out, waving a paddle in the air.

"Grab a canoe," Rusty yelled.

A feeling of joy swept over me. I ran to a canoe, jumped in, and paddled to catch up with the guys.

As I glided up alongside the three canoes, Mark called out. "OK. Stop paddling. It's time for the gunwale jumping world championship race."

Mark stowed his paddle in the bottom of his canoe. In steady motions, he stood on the rear thwart, bent over, placing his hands on the sides of the canoe, then placed his feet behind his hands in a compact crouched position, and stood. Standing on the sides or gunwales at the rear of the canoe, he bent his knees then pushed down hard, causing the bow of the canoe to rise out of the water then splash down. He repeated his knee bending gyrations, making the front of the canoe lift and splash, lift and splash, several times in a row. The motion caused the canoe to lurch forward with each splash.

Rusty and Tim stood on their canoes mimicking the gunwale jumping movements, forcing their canoes to jerk across the water, sending waves rippling behind them.

I paddled several strokes ahead, then copied their movements, placing my hands and feet on the gunwales, but I felt spread out like a daddy long-leg spider. I tried to stand, but felt myself falling forward. Keeping my feet in place, I moved one hand back, then the next, clawing at the gunwales, scrunching my body until my center of gravity was over my hips. Finally, I stood, balancing awkwardly on the narrow edges of the canoe.

The boat rocked under my wobbly legs. Bending my knees slightly, I pushed down. The front of the canoe rose, then dipped in the water. The canoe barely moved, but I was doing it. I smiled, feeling confident. Bending my knees again, then pushing down, the canoe splashed forward.

As I was getting the hang of the motion, Rusty and Tim passed me, gunwale jumping with full force. The bows of their canoes lifted three feet off the water and splashed down hard, sending wakes from their crashing bows into the side of my canoe. The narrow boat rocked under my unsteady legs. I lost my balance and fell in the water.

The boys laughed as I breast stroked to my canoe. "Did you see him fly?" Tim asked.

"He almost did a back flip," shouted Rusty.

"That sounds like fun," Mark said. He then back flipped off the back of his canoe, rotating fully, landing in the water feet first. Not to be left out, Tim and Rusty attempted back flips off their canoes. Tim landed on his back with a slapping sound, howling in pain. Rusty went in headfirst, sending his canoe skimming away.

The boys swam to their canoes, lifted themselves in and stood on the gunwales as if it was the normal position from which to navigate a canoe.

"Line up with my canoe at the starting line. Time for the race," Mark said. Four canoes lined up in the middle of Siltcoos lake. The blue-green water rippled in the coastal breeze, glimmering with reflections of the summer sun as we stood astride our watercraft.

"Ready, set, go." Mark shouted.

We pushed, pumping our legs furiously, rocking our boats across the water in heated competition. Mark was quickly out in front, with Rusty just behind. I got off to a slow start, but soon gained speed as I discovered the rhythm.

Pushing hard, forcing the rear of my canoe deep into the water, the bow rose, then I lifted my arms and bent my knees, allowing the aft of the canoe to rise as the bow splashed down, sending water spraying across my body.

Joyously, I looked out across the lake with the sun on my face and the wind in my hair. I rode the canoe hard, pushing again and again, perfecting my timing as the canoe staggered forward, gaining momentum. I waved as I passed Tim, who was tiring.

Rusty was a boat length ahead, working to keep up with Mark. The movement of my canoe smoothed with the steady motion, moving gracefully through the water. My canoe inched closer to Rusty's with each piston like push of my legs. Soon I was cruising next to Rusty, our bodies alternating up and down, canoes lifting and splashing, both gaining on Mark. When the bows of our canoes nudged alongside of Mark's, he stopped pushing.

"I win," Mark shouted, standing tall on his canoe as it glided across the water, his arms stretched to the sky.

"What?" I shouted.

"We were about to pass you," said Rusty.

"It can't be over yet," I said.

"It's a quarter mile race. Look how far we went. I win," Mark said, pointing.

"That's not fair. I could have beat you," I said.

"But you didn't. I won."

"How do you know it was a quarter mile?" Rusty asked.

"I know this lake. That was a quarter mile, probably more. My race. My rules."

Tim caught up to us and floated next to Mark. "Cheater," Tim yelled, jumping from his canoe, tackling Mark, sending them both in the water. Rusty and I dove in to help Tim wrestle Mark as we splashed and dunked each other. We spent the afternoon paddling, gunwale jumping and swamping each other's canoes.

Chapter Seventeen

That night, after we'd served the camp staff dinner, we heard a loud commotion in the dining hall. "Why do you suspect me?" I heard Mark complain. The kitchen crew and I pushed through the swinging door to see what was happening. Mr. Donaldson and Marty Sawyer, the adult leader who ran the trading post, were talking to Mark by the fireplace. "I didn't do it. I'm not a thief," Mark protested.

There were words spoken that we could not hear. "Yes. I was there, so were twenty other scouts buying snacks."

Brian joined the men surrounding Mark. "What did you do now?"

"Screw you, Brian. You always assume I'm guilty. Aren't you supposed to support me?"

Mr. Donaldson looked sternly at Brian, then at Mark. "Son, fess up. Things will go easier for you."

"I told you. I am not a thief."

Marty pointed an accusatory finger at Mark. "I had four twenty-dollar bills in the till. You were standing next to the register. After you left, the twenties were gone."

"You've got to be kidding. I was at the register paying."

We walked closer and heard Mr. Donaldson. "Come to my office. We'll wait for the police and let them decide."

"The police. No fucking way."

"Settle down," Brian said.

Marty made a move to grab hold of Mark. "Get your hands off me. You have no right. I didn't do anything."

Mark pushed Marty and ran out of the dining hall.

"Mark, come back. This isn't solving anything." Brian yelled.

"Only the guilty run, boy." Marty called out.

Mark leaped off the porch and ran up the road.

"The County Sheriff will be here soon. We'll let him deal with this," said Donaldson.

I marched up the aisle between tables, shouting. "You don't even know him. You think he's a criminal cause you watched the nightly news? Mark would never steal. Do you have any evidence? What proof do you have?"

"Calm down, son. This is none of your business," Mr. Donaldson said.

I was livid. "Brian, you remember. Mark wouldn't help that cheating Mr. Bevins forge merit badge cards. Mark refused to lie. What makes you think he's a thief?"

Marty tried to grab hold of me, but I pulled away. "Did you even ask Mark if he took the money, or did you just assume and accuse him?"

Marty looked puzzled. "He's been in trouble before. Who else?"

"Danny, go back to the kitchen," Brian ordered.

"No. I'm defending my friend. It's more than you're doing."

The way the men treated Mark was brutally unfair. Now I understood what Mark said about everyone looking at him and seeing a criminal without ever taking a moment to know him.

"So, what will you tell the police, Marty? There were twenty kids in the store. Money went missing and you accuse a boy because you saw him on TV. Did you know the police never charged Mark with a crime? Yet, you see a criminal."

Mr. Donaldson looked concerned. "Is that true Marty? Did you see Mark take the money?"

Marty shrunk. "No. He was there. It was the logical conclusion."

"But not factual. You have no witness."

"Well, no."

Mr. Donaldson looked disappointed.

I stepped toward Mr. Donaldson. "We've got to find Mark. He said he can't take being seen as a crook anymore. Now you've called the police on him."

"Do you think Mark might hurt himself?" Donaldson asked.

"If you consider spending eternity in the ocean swimming with fishes hurting himself, then yes."

"You think he'd go to the ocean?"

"He talked about it before."

Mr. Donaldson waved over the adult leaders, who were watching keenly. "We'll form a search party. I assume Mark is headed for the dunes. We need to get him before he reaches the ocean. Get your cars over there. I consider the boy innocent. Got that? We've spooked him with an unproven accusation. We're searching to protect Mark Colby."

Brian waved. "Waterfront staff with me."

I understood why Mark ran. He ran from the police. The ones who debased him, made him less than. The ones who put the stink of crime on him. An odor he couldn't shake. People smelled it wherever he went. They sensed the fetid stench, pointing accusing fingers. He ran from people who assumed he was guilty when he deserved none of the guilt. He ran to find peace.

It takes longer than you'd expect to get a group of people moving in the same direction. We were about to leave when the County Sherriff arrived. While Mr. Donaldson and Marty talked with the sheriff, Tim, Rusty, Dennis, Eric, Tony, and I climbed into Brian's old Ford Bronco. Tony and I sat behind the backseat in the cramped cargo area.

The Oregon dunes are the largest expanse of coastal sand dunes in North America, covering 7,000 acres, with some dunes reaching 500 feet above sea level. When Brian parked, we piled out of the Bronco facing a golden mountain and a river of sand that spilled down to the highway.

"Spread out. Cover as much area as we can." Brian yelled after us as we began climbing. My shoes sank in the soft, shifting sand, filling them with silicon grains cascading over my feet as I climbed the steep wall of sand.

This spot next to the highway was directly across from Clear Lake Road, the road leading to Camp Baker, and a popular stop for families. Hundreds of footprints tracked up the steep dune. It was impossible to tell if Mark had come this way, but we climbed.

We made our way up the initial slope, then came to a gradually rising plateau of sand bordered by an area of low shrubs. Most of the guys stayed on the plateau, the river of sand, but I stuck close to the western edge of crumbling dirt and low grass that led to a tree island, a group of trees and shrubs surrounded by sand that ran up to a prominent ridge. Climbing through the hard sand and scruffy vegetation was easier than slogging through the deep sand.

Climbing to the crest of the shrub covered hill, I stood under gray overcast skies. Misty wind hit my face. It wasn't raining. It took a lot more than a few drops of mist to register as rain with an Oregon kid. It surprised me that the dunes weren't an endless vastness of golden sand stretching to the sea like I'd seen in the movies.

Instead, the sand rolled away unevenly, and water filled the low-lying areas of the transverse dunes, forming ponds and lakes. In the distance were trees, a large island of scrub that somehow had not succumbed to the wind and sand.

I stood on the crest and yelled. "Mark. Mark." The wind swept my voice away with the mist. I ran down the slope of sand, short grass, and shrubs to the rolling plain where the sand was harder. I saw Tony running across undulating hills of sand in the distance. He raised his hands to his mouth. Wisps of his words carried with the wind reached my ears as hollow tones.

Moving over the rising and falling terrain, stopping often to scream his name, walking up a ridge to skirt around a large pond, I edged my way toward the distant tree island. A person could move out there crossing over the rolling mounds, long ridges and wind cut swoops and, like a ship bobbing up and down on swells in the sea, you could easily miss sight of them.

I spotted something, a glimpse, a passing image on a distant rising swell, but just as quickly, it went out of sight. I could've waited to see if it would rise again, but I rushed to the crest of a sandbank and saw the glimpse was only a trick of light. Refusing to be defeated, I called out again. The wind was colder, stronger, and the skies getting darker. Grains of sand, whipped by the wind, stung my eyes, but I pushed on, ever forward, searching, calling his name.

Another called now, cutting through the damp wind. The squelch of a bull horn marked arrival of the greater search party. Looking back, I saw the silhouettes of men on the high shrub lined ridge, ready to start their search.

I went down a slope and walked across a low, dark area of crunchy dried sand. A spot that in winter had been a pond but was now dried by the summer sun. I liked the feel and sound of the crunchy crisp sand crackling under my feet.

The island was closer now. I thought I saw movement in the thick trees and called again. "Mark. Mark. They know it wasn't you. Mark." I thought I saw him turn toward my voice just before I fell through the crunchy sand.

Down I went into a deep, damp sand pit. I clawed furiously at the sides, trying to climb out, but the sand wall crumbled, burying my legs. I tried to pull my feet loose and lost a shoe. Digging at the sand, I tried to climb, but the pit caved in around me. The more I struggled to pull myself free, the deeper I went, bringing more sand down around me.

"Help, help. Please somebody, help." I cried. My efforts to pull myself out of the cold, heavy sand exhausted me. I was breathing hard, feeling the weight of damp sand press down on me as darkness fell. "Help," I called weakly.

All the times I struggled with chores, hoping that someone would come and rescue me from my dreary life, came back to me. No matter how hard I had wished, no one ever came. My life really sucked now. Buried up to my chest, as the dark wet sand squeezed the breath out of me, I realized no one would ever come. It was time to let go of childhood fantasies and magical thinking. It was time to let go. Time to go.

No one saw me. I was in the trough of a swell, lost in a sea of sand, and I would not rise on that swell again. Moving to make room to breathe, I sunk. The sand was up to my neck. All I could think was that if I was lost and buried here, my mom would save money on my funeral. Wind swirled in my pit, sending evil dancing sprites of sand to sting my face, nose, and ears. My eyes closed.

Only the top of my head and three fingers of one hand were visible when Mark found me. "Danny. Hang on. I'll get you out." Mark laid on his stomach across the dark pit and pulled the sand away from my nose and mouth. Scooping with both hands like a breaststroke pull, he moved sand, flinging it behind him.

"I'll get you out. Don't worry," he said scoop after scoop. When he was tired, he rolled over on his back and shouted for help, then rolled back and dug again.

Tony was the next to arrive. He dropped to his knees and started digging. "Tony, lay down to distribute your body weight," Mark instructed. Tony got on his stomach and dug.

A few minutes later. "What the hell?" Dennis asked. He stood watching for a moment. "How did he do that? It's not even giant sand crab season, yet." Instead of dropping on his stomach to dig, Dennis ran away.

Mark glanced at Tony while scooping frantically, "Where's that lazy ass run off to?"

"Dennis. Why aren't you helping?" Tony screamed.

"Dig," Mark yelled, pulling at the sand like a madman.

The sound of a wailing siren cut through the chill wind. The sight of Dennis jumping, waving his arms through the mist, pointing to our crisis, brought sudden hope.

"County Search and Rescue. They came out for Mark. They can save Danny," Dennis shouted. Seconds later, the search and rescue men swarmed in, pulling an oxygen mask over my face.

They yelled at Mark and Tony to stop. "Move back. We'll handle it from here, boys." Tony scrambled away, but Mark kept digging.

"I've got to get him out," Mark said, digging at the sand. The rescue men grabbed Mark and moved him away from the dark sand pit so they could place long planks around me. Mark collapsed on the sand; his body spent. "He's got to be OK. Save him. Please save him."

I coughed in the mask and opened my eyes. One man checked me and gave a thumbs up. Another man secured a rope around my body, under my armpits. I was utterly helpless as the men worked. I was numb, my body void, one with the cold hard sand. The men dug carefully, as if sculpting an emerging form out of marble. Chiseling away, slowly, my sand coated body took shape. Shovels dug behind my body until I fell backward.

"Relax. Lean back slowly now, like you're floating," the man said.

Two of the men dug at the front of me, cautious of my buried legs while the other men held the rope. Slowly, they pulled me, fully formed, out of that dark pit.

I sat on the sand breathing oxygen while a medic checked my vitals. I looked around and everyone from the waterfront and the adult staff were there. Brian talked quietly as Mark nodded his head slowly, then Brian hugged him. Mr. Donaldson walked over to Mark, said a few words, then shook his hand.

"He checks out fine," the medic announced. "He's lucky someone got to him quickly. A few more minutes and this would have ended differently." He asked me if I could stand. I nodded. The man grabbed me under an armpit and helped me to my feet. As I stood, sand streamed off me. Dark, sticky grains coated my arms, face, and clothes.

I removed the oxygen mask and thanked everyone.

There was talk of sending me to the hospital, but my vitals were good, and I had no broken bones. The last thing I wanted was to spend the night in a hospital room or get sent home.

Search and Rescue drove me and the waterfront crew to the small parking area. My attitude seemed to gain respect from the search and rescue team as I thanked each one. "I'll shake it off," I said, then I climbed into the front passenger seat of Brian's Bronco.

What I really wanted was a hot shower.

Some wishes come true. When we got back to camp, Mr. Farnsworth, the caretaker, had the boiler in the shower house fired and the water running hot. I walked into the shower fully clothed. Dark muddy sand streamed off me and flowed down the drain. The blackness of death swirled at my feet. Slowly, I stripped off my shirt and pants. I took my time scrubbing the grit away, allowing the hot rain to caress and warm my body. Sand had worked its way into every fold, crevasse, and hole in my body. I washed out my clothes, wrung them dry, and tossed them on a wooden bench. Then I rinsed myself again.

Standing in front of a mirror with a towel around my waist, I observed my body. Turning slowly to the right and left, I flexed my leanly muscled arms and chest, then ran a hand over my hard, flat stomach.

Eric startled me when he appeared in the mirror behind me. "Hey Danny, I brought you a change of clothes." He looked at my reflection. "Looks like all that swimming and rowing is paying off."

Embarrassed, I turned away from the mirror. "Can you call me Dan from now on? Danny sounds like a kid's name."

"Sure. I'll call you Dan. Dan-O. Dan-Dan. Super Dan, or Dan the man, but never call you Danny, again."

I took the clothes from Eric. "Thanks, man."

Chapter Eighteen

A few nights after my near-death experience, I found Mark sitting on the dining hall steps after dinner cleanup. I had spent little time with him since he'd saved my life. Not for any reason. It was a busy week. The camp was full of scouts and mom had scheduled extra shifts for me in the kitchen. I think she wanted to keep an eye on me.

Besides, after what happened, I felt like spending some time alone. In the evenings I'd walk down dark trails listening to the forest, hoping the giant old trees had some wisdom to share or I'd stand on the lake shore gazing at the stars, wondering what was out there. I thought maybe almost dying would bring a better understanding of life, but it hadn't. God didn't speak to me. The blinking stars weren't transmitting secret morse code messages and trees don't talk, or if they do, they speak so slowly it takes greater patience than I had to hear what they have to say.

There was nothing. No special meaning, no encoded messages. Life picked up where it left off and continued as if the dark pit of death hadn't swallowed me. Life went on, flowing like a river sweeping me up, carrying me with the current of daily life, the routine of working in the kitchen and spending afternoons on the waterfront teaching crazy young boys to canoe, but I very much hoped that somehow, I would discover something more.

Mark sat on the steps looking up at me. "Are you okay? How are you feeling?"

"I'm fine." I didn't know what else to say. "My chest hurts a bit if I take a deep breath. Otherwise, I'm just like new."

"I heard you want to be called Dan now."

"Yeah."

"All right, I'll call you Dan, but you'll always be a weird little freak to me," he said with a smile.

"Are you waiting for me?"

"Who else would I be waiting for?"

"I don't know. Tim or Dennis. Rusty, maybe."

"Nah."

There was silence for a moment. Maybe it was my melancholy mood.

"Hey, you want to go for a ride?"

"Riding what?"

"A dirt bike."

"Who has a dirt bike around here?"

"Mr. Farnsworth. It was his son's. He lets me take it out when I need to get away."

"Are you sure? Is that why you were chopping wood? Punishment for taking his dirt bike?"

"I was chopping wood to help him, like I told you. We help each other. I chop wood. He lets me use the bike. Fair and square."

Mark started walking. "Come on. It's a blast."

"You're sure we won't get in trouble."

"I guarantee it."

We walked to the caretaker's house. The night was warm and there was a full moon rising in the darkening sky.

"Wait here," Mark said, then ran to the garage, entering through a side door. A few seconds later, he came out pushing a motorbike. He ran with it, pushing it down the road. I ran after him. He stopped when we reached the parking lot. "Why'd you push it all the way here?"

"Mr. Farnsworth sleeps early. I don't want the engine to wake him."

The bike was sporty, with knobby tires and long front forks with a raised fender. The burnt orange gas tank had YAMAHA printed on it, and ENDURO 250 emblazoned on the battery cover, painted the same color. "Are you sure we can ride it?"

Mark reached into his pocket. "I've got my own key," he said, holding up a pair of nail clippers.

"That's not a key."

"It works like a key." Mark opened the lever of the nail clippers, inserted it into the key slot and twisted it to the ON position. He put his leg over the saddle, straddling the bike, then put his foot on the kick starter and pressed down hard, turning the engine's piston as he twisted the throttle. The bike roared to life.

"Get on," he directed.

I put my left foot on the rear footrest and threw my right leg over the saddle. My foot found the other footrest, and I sat on the black vinyl seat behind Mark.

I'd been on dirt bikes many times. Lots of kids' families owned dirt bikes where I lived. I'd even rode one by myself a few times. There were trails along the river and in the hills. Growing up in Lebanon, I might not get exposed to news of the world or get cultured. I'd never vacationed in Italy, or watched porn, but I rode dirt bikes.

"Hang on." Mark shouted over the sound of the revving engine. I wrapped my arms around his waist. He used his foot to click into first gear and we were off.

Mark drove slowly out of camp, then turned north on Clear Lake Road past houses, pastures, and trees for a couple of miles, gliding on the smooth paved road. I held tight with my chest at his back, my arms around his waist, my chin on his shoulder, the crisp evening air blowing in my face, and through my hair. He rode with confidence around a wide turn as a lake came into view, its silver slate surface reflecting the moon. "Is that Siltcoos?" I asked, my mouth at his ear.

"No, that's Woahink."

I recalled that Woahink Lake lies just north of Siltcoos. When we came to a turn, I noticed the sign read Schrum Creek Road, but it wasn't much of a road. After a few hundred feet, the pavement ended, and the road became a single lane dirt track. Now far from homes, surrounded by forest, Mark revved the engine, increasing speed, the throaty exhaust thrumming with each change of gear.

"Lots of logging roads in these hills,' Mark said, shouting over the sound of the engine. The old dirt road weaved uphill. When we came to a long straight a-way, Mark called out, "Hang on," just before he popped a wheelie. I tightened my grip as I felt gravity pulling me back. I held on for dear life as the Enduro raced down the road, zipping past trees on one wheel. Mark dropped back down on two wheels when we approached a section of winding road that took us higher into the hills.

We rode down logging roads and rutted single lane dirt tracks, the rising moon peeking through gaps in trees. I sat behind him in silent meditation as the cool wind whipped at my shirt. The chill was all around me, but Mark's body radiated heat, keeping me warm.

Holding tight, I became one with the engine's vibration, barreling down logging roads through the night, feeling that time had ceased. I didn't know where we were going and didn't care. We were free, far from our paltry existence. The pain of life swept behind us like so much dust. I understood why Mark liked to ride. The sound of the whining engine washed my worries away.

After a time, the cycle slowed as Mark downshifted. He killed the engine, letting the bike drift silently into a misty Moon lit meadow. Wispy fog hung over a brilliant white garden glen. Under our feet, a bed of white clover stretched across the dale, to white flowering dogwood trees circling the meadow.

I stood at the bike full of wonder as Mark walked to the center of the white carpeted glade. Moon beams illuminated the swirling mist as he held out his arms and fell back into the thick, soft clover.

Stepping through the meadow, I marveled at the beauty of snowy white flowers at my feet and blossoming dogwood trees, their tender white petals lit by moonlight like dew dripped crystals. I fell back with my arms spread wide, landing softly on the downy bed of sweet clover, my fingers inches from his. Breathing deeply, I absorbed the sweet floral nectar.

"Is this heaven?" I asked.

"If it's not, it's damn near."

I was silent, lost in thought for a moment. "Thanks for saving my life."

"You scared the shit out of me. I thought you were dead."

"Does that mean we're friends?"

Mark rolled to his side and looked me in the eye. "I wouldn't have dug you out if you weren't my friend. "

"No kidding?"

Mark turned his eyes to the bright full moon. "You're the best friend I've ever had."

I stared at the mean older boy who said we'd never be friends. "I think you're the only real friend I've ever had."

We laid in sweet clover surrounded by white dogwood blossoms, staring at a night sky filled with twinkling stars.

Finally, I said, "It feels weird not dying."

"What do you mean?"

Inhaling the floral scented air, I wondered how I was supposed to feel about surviving that dark pit?

"I don't know. I was nearly dead. You saved me, then I wasn't."

"You're welcome."

"I survived. I'm alive and life goes on, like almost dying was nothing more than a bump in the road. No big deal. Like it wouldn't matter if I was alive or dead. Either way, life goes on."

"Aren't you glad you're alive?"

"Sure. I just feel it should mean something."

"Maybe you need to give it time. My uncle used to say that for life to have meaning, we must suffer pain. We seek pleasure, but the struggles in our life are what define us. Adversity molds us. A meaningful life develops out of suffering. Living a simple life with no difficulties, no challenges, or pain sounds nice, but it's empty. A life of meaning comes from a life of suffering."

"I guess almost dying counts as suffering."

"Yeah, I'd say so. Give yourself time, you'll figure it out."

"Your uncle was a smart guy. Do you still miss him?"

"I miss him every day."

I fell asleep lying on soft white flowers under the moonlit sky, impatient for suffering to bring meaning to my life.

Chapter Nineteen

It's easy to forget your worries when your days are busy working in the kitchen, watching energetic scouts run down forest trails, basking in the summer sun, swimming, and boating. After a few days, my somber mood, like gray clouds of an overcast sky, burned away with the summer sun.

It was a warm, lazy Saturday afternoon in staff camp. I sat in a chair outside my cabin reading The Hobbit. Kurt lent me the book after being shocked to learn I had never heard of J. R. R. Tolkien or his books. Kurt felt it was a sacrilege I had not read Tolkien and hastened to fix my ignorance, insisting I read The Hobbit.

I paused the adventure of Bilbo Baggins' journey to the Misty Mountains to study the sunlight filtering through the trees rustling in the breeze. I viewed the camp's broad forest floor, its cabins scattered amongst the trees, the old picnic table, and fire pit surrounded by logs, all gently sloping to the lake. These surroundings gave me a deep feeling of contentment.

As I lazed in my chair, Mark came out of his cabin and ran across the camp. "Hey, where are you going?" I asked, calling out to him.

"For a run. Want to come along?"

"You jog? I didn't think you could survive out of the water."

"Running through the forest is a nice change of pace. You up for a run?"

I was not a runner. In my P.E. class at the end of the school year, we were required to run a mile in under twelve minutes. I finished in eleven minutes, fifty-five seconds.

"I'll go, as long as you don't run like Steve Prefontaine."

"Nah, I'll take it easy on you."

I ran to my cabin, kicked off my thongs, pulled on my black swim trunks to use as jogging shorts and laced up my Converse tennis shoes.

When I reappeared, Mark started off in a slow jog down the slope toward the lake. I ran to catch up. "Where are we headed?"

Mark didn't answer. He went south, down a narrow trail that traced the shoreline. I ran behind him as he followed the trail wherever it led; along the water's edge, swerving inland up an incline, tracking over uneven terrain, then back along the jagged shoreline.

I felt free running through the forest breathing in the crisp sweet air, hopping over roots crossing the trail. We weaved through trees, around tall flowering rhododendron, and bushy thickets, jumped over fallen logs, then down the slope back to the water's edge where tiny waves broke, lapping against the shore.

Mark kept a steady pace, but not so fast that I couldn't keep up. The trail took us sharply inland around a cove where we passed through vacant camps. Without scouts or tents, the camps comprised empty picnic tables, burned out firepits, and flattened grass where tents had stood earlier that day. It was odd seeing the camps empty, knowing that boys had slept and played there hours before. The boys had gone home, but I sensed their lingering energy.

When we entered a campsite named Captain Gray, I plopped down on the picnic table, breathing hard. Mark stood bent over with his hands on his knees, catching his breath. "You hanging in there?" he asked.

"I think I prefer swimming." I pulled off my t-shirt and used it to wipe sweat from my face. Mark pulled off his shirt, exposing his smooth muscled chest, wiped his face, and tucked the shirt in the back of his shorts, hanging like a tail.

"Want to keep going?"

"Sure. I've never been this far down the western shore," I said, tucking my t-shirt behind me, unsure how much further I could go.

We ran with our shirts off down an overgrown trail that smelled of old wood heading south, running past gigantic trees that had massive wide trunks with roots three feet tall at their base spreading out across the forest floor. Mark easily navigated the dark trail hopscotching roots and jumping over fallen trees like a young gazelle. I marveled at how his strong sinewy legs moved so nimbly through the undergrowth, the fern, and huckleberry nipping at his ankles. I imagined we were the first humans to travel through this ancient land, but then we ran through a camp named Conestoga, and later Applegate, and realized we were not the first humans to set foot in this place.

The trail took us back to the lake; the path hugging the shoreline until the terrain flattened, and the trail grew wider. For the first time, we ran side by side. "How far are we going?" I asked, breathing hard.

"The end of the peninsula isn't much farther. You think we can make it?"

"I think so, but I'll probably walk back." There was no way I'd admit it, but I was dead tired. I would never have run this far if Mark wasn't pulling me along, but I didn't want to give up and look like a wimp.

"Salmon berries," Mark shouted, stopping at a bramble of dark green leaves, stems covered with small sharp prickles, and fruit that resembled yellow-orange raspberries. Mark picked and ate the small berries.

I stood in front of the thicket of orange berries, panting. "Thank God."

"The perfect treat for the end of a run," Mark said, stuffing berries in his mouth.

I ate the warm sour sweet fruit heated by the sun, melting in my mouth like berries baked in a pie. I held a berry up to the sun, observing the deep orange color of the round drupelets reminding me of salmon eggs.

"Did you ever eat a salmon egg?" I asked.

"No."

"I ate one once. Nearly puked. These look exactly like tiny salmon eggs."

"Why would you eat a salmon egg?"

"One time, one of my mom's boyfriends took me and my brother fishing. I guess he was trying to impress her or act like a father figure. He brought a bunch of fishing gear and taught us how to use a rod and reel. He used salmon eggs from a grody glass jar as bait. I didn't want to fish. It was boring standing in the scorching sun, hoping to catch a fish. Billy loved fishing. He did everything he could to get the man's approval, and the chump sucked it up, encouraging Billy. I tossed my pole to the ground and sat in the shade.

"The guy asked me if I would fish if he ate a salmon egg. They looked gross, so I said, deal. Dang, if he didn't stick his finger in that yucky jar, pull out an egg and pop it in his mouth with a smile. It didn't seem like much of a challenge. I felt gypped. It told him I'd eat one if he'd give me five bucks. He agreed if I promised to fish. He handed me the half-empty jar that had been baking in the sun. The eggs smelled like rotten fish.

"I dug a finger into the slimy jar, rolled one of the round orange eggs up the side of the dirty glass until I could grab it with two fingers. Holding the warm egg in front of my mouth. I asked again to confirm our bet. Five bucks?

"The man nodded. I popped the egg into my mouth and chewed. Warm, putrid slime gushed over my tongue. It tasted horrible. I spit it out, choking and gagging. Billy laughed at me."

"Did he pay you the five bucks?"

"No, because I spit it out. He said my mistake was chewing it. I hate fishing."

"And salmon eggs."

"Yes, but salmon berries I can eat all day," I said, popping a berry into my mouth.

"Look over there," Mark said. Ahead of us, at the water's edge, was a giant western red cedar with two extra trunks swooping over the ground, then turning upward toward the sky.

"They look like elephant tusks," I said.

"The elephant tree."

We ran to the tree, climbing up the thick curving lower trunk. Mark and I sat cradled along the length of the swooping limb face to face, his shoes pressed against mine, bracing ourselves on the giant tusk.

I looked across the water. There were two islands, a small one, two hundred yards offshore, and a larger island further out. The western shore was far beyond the islands, where the small community of Dunes

City dotted the shoreline with small resorts and marinas. It amazed me that people loved this lake enough to live here and build holiday homes.

It made me think of the future, a mysterious thing you try to imagine, but can never see.

I looked at Mark. Locks of his long black hair hung over his dark eyes. "What do you want to be when you grow up?"

He leaned back against the tree trunk in thought before saying, "I want to be a lawyer."

I'd never thought about anyone wanting to be a lawyer. "Why a lawyer?"

"When I was in Skipworth, the detention center, I had a public defender, Mr. Evans. He did everything he could to help me. He came to visit twice a week. Even after the district attorney dropped the charges, he came to check on me. I'd like to help kids in trouble like Mr. Evans. What do you want to be?"

"I don't know. I want to earn enough money to eat at fancy restaurants, live in a new house, drive a cool car, own a laser sailboat, and have a bank account with fifty thousand dollars."

"That would make you happy?"

"I think so."

"And three big dogs?" Mark asked, smiling.

"No dogs. Maybe a wife and a couple of kids. I can teach them to swim and sail."

"Sounds like a great life. I hope you'll invite me to go sailing."

"I will. Do you think it's possible? Can we have good lives? Better than our parents?"

"I hope so if we can keep from fucking it up."

"My parents fucked up their lives. Sometimes I think my life is doomed to fail."

"My uncle John said, life is what you make it. You create your own destiny."

"And he got murdered."

Mark looked sad. I instantly regretted saying that. "Sorry."

"Yeah, well, you can only do your best, right? You're going to be okay, Dan Novak."

"You think so?"

"I do."

"You're gonna be a great lawyer."

Chapter Twenty

It was jamboree week. There was no National Scout Jamboree that year, so a series of special events took place for scouts at Camp Baker. Scout troops and visitors occupied every camp on the peninsula. We'd set up special tents in the assembly area where old men wearing scout uniforms traded patches like rare stamps. A new zip line in the pioneering area ran from the top of a tall climbing tower through the trees ending at a pile of sawdust, there was an overnight camp to the sand dunes, a special campfire show with a music group, a comedian all the way from Portland, and the mile swim.

The August sun in Oregon is hot. Clouds blown inland from the Pacific Ocean evaporate into wisps of white fluff dissolving over the lake. I rowed with my back to Mark, who sat relaxing in the bow. Once we were in the middle of the lake, I stowed the oars and let the boat drift. Mark's body stretched across the wide wooden bow thwart with his head resting on one gunwale, his feet hanging over the other.

I laid on the stern thwart. Two boys relaxing on the placid lake. The sun beat down, causing beads of sweat to well up on my browning skin. A length of rope in a loose coil attached to a rusty anchor sat on the floor of the wooden boat. Mark disturbed the peace by throwing the anchor in the water with a heavy plunk. I watched the rope play out until the anchor hit bottom.

"Race you to the railroad trestle on the far shore and back. Loser rows back to camp."

"Deal," I said, stretching slowly.

Mark dove in and swam. "Hey. You didn't say go," I squealed, diving after him. We swam, leaving the rowboat bobbing in the water, the anchor keeping company with the sturgeon's and eels.

We raced across the lake toward the distant railroad trestles. After several minutes, Mark made the old piling first. He touched the wood and turned. I followed closely, made the turn, and grabbed the water, pulling at it, then pushing the fluid past my hips as I kicked, before reaching out to grip the water stroke after stroke until I was pulling ahead of Mark. He kicked harder and pulled faster to match my pace.

I repeated the swim mantra Mark had taught me to keep my mind focused on my stroke and sight my course. With each breath on my right-side I saw Mark swimming powerfully. I increased my speed until I was a body length ahead. I made it back to the boat first, panting and breathing hard. Mark touched the boat seconds later, gasping for air.

"You little fuck. You've been holding out on me. I've earned so many mile swim badges, they quit giving them to me, and you beat my ass," he said, panting.

I glowed, happy to receive Mark's praise. "Want to go again? I'll go easy on you next time."

"Screw you, runt," Mark said, pulling himself into the boat.

I grabbed the transom, kicked once, and pressed down in a single powerful motion to exit the water and stepped into the boat. I stood tall, shaking the water off me like a dog, trying to splash Mark.

"Look at you. You must have grown six inches this summer." He threw his head back, tossing back his shaggy summer length hair, then jerked his head forward, spraying me with water droplets.

I shielded myself from the spray. "I'm almost as tall as you."

"Guess I can't call you a little runt anymore."

Mark rowed with long slow strokes, staring at me as I laid across the stern thwart lazily dragging my fingers in the water.

"Not afraid of the sturgeons and eels anymore?"

"When I'm with you, I'm not afraid of anything," I said innocently, watching the water ripple and swirl around my fingertips.

Mark stood, flexing his muscles. "I am Poseidon's son, protector of the seven seas and all the creatures within. The ocean is my temple.

Nothing can harm those under my protection. I give you Poseidon's promise."

I laughed. "With that long hair, you look more like the swamp creature. What movie is that Poseidon thing from?"

"It's not from a movie. It's my promise. I feel best when I'm in the water. Free from judgement, one with the swirling tide, and it, one with me. Sometimes I imagine I'm Poseidon's son and dream about how great it would be to live in the ocean, protector of the sea." Mark sat and stared at me for a long while. "Swamp Creature? Is that what you think?"

"Is that a real promise?"

"I told you before, it's my superpower. You'll always be under my protection whenever you're in the water."

"I wish I had a superpower."

"From what I just saw, swimming is your superpower."

"Yeah? Then I'm glad the mile swim is tomorrow," I said.

"Now I get it. You've been holding back until the day before the big swim, then you beat me. Looks like I'll have some competition this year."

"Brian should be happy, and you'll be off punishment."

Mark scanned the lake, observing the blue sky and the green trees along the shoreline. "If this is punishment, give me a life sentence. It was punishment for you, too. He forced you to spend every afternoon on the lake with me."

"Yeah, that sucked. I've hated every minute," I said, laughing.

"We should talk to Brian. Let him know you're ready."

"Cool swamp creature."

"You'd better come up with something better than swamp creature before I pound you."

Mark and I stood in Brian and Molly's tent. Molly lounged in a cushioned chair with her arms wrapped around her enormous bulging belly. I worried that if she let go, the unborn twins would spill out onto the floor.

Brian noticed us staring at Molly's huge belly.

"I did that. It's my fault, and I'd do it again in a heartbeat, even though she's been cursing me all summer."

"Look what you did to me. I'm huge. I'll be blaming you for the next twenty years."

"It's amazing. It really works," Brian said as he made a hand gesture. One hand with his thumb and index finger touching to make a circle and the index finger of his other hand moving in and out of the hole. He looked at us, smiling. "Get it, huh? Get it?" he asked, making the gesture again.

I gave an embarrassed nod.

"Yeah, we get it Brian," said Mark.

"I'm ready for the mile swim," I blurted out.

"The race is tomorrow morning. You'd better damned well be ready. Mark, can he make it?"

"He'll make it. We raced to the far shore and back today. He beat me by a couple seconds and he's still swimming in those," Mark said, pointing at my baggy waterfront shorts.

Brian looked me over. "Those shorts create lots of drag. You'd swim faster if you wore a racing suit."

"That's what I was thinking. He's earned it."

"Mark, check the box. See if there's one his size," Brian said.

Mark rummaged through a cardboard box at the back of the tent.

"He's been here every day, earned every waterfront merit badge, and he's been teaching the sailing and canoeing classes," Mark added.

Mark pulled a red Speedo racing suit from the box and handed it to me.

"The racing suits are only for full-time waterfront staff, but it sounds like you deserve it," Brian said.

Molly smiled. "Good for you Danny." Molly still called me Danny. I didn't mind.

"Wow, thanks," I said, admiring the small nylon suit.

"If you swim like Mark says, you'll be even faster wearing that," Brian said.

"Wear it always. Poseidon commands it," Mark said in a deep voice.

"Whatever you say, swamp man," I said.

Brian scrunched his face. "You guys are weird. Must be the comic books you boys read these days. Those things will rot your brain. The mile swim starts tomorrow at seven a.m. Don't be late. Now get out of here. I have a hot, sweaty pregnant wife who needs my attention, unless you want to stay and watch."

Mark and I ran out of the tent screaming.

That night in the dining hall

Mr. Donaldson stood in front of the fireplace. "Before I dismiss you, I have an important announcement. Tonight, as a special part of jamboree week, there will be a rare ceremony for a select group of scouts. We will induct new members into the Order of the Silver Bow. This is a special honor because you cannot earn your way into the Order of the Silver Bow like you earn a merit badge. The Silver Bow is not about what you do, but about who you are. Your fellow scouts chose the potential members of this order. Candidates are selected based on their honor, courage, and leadership skills. Members of the Silver Bow become leaders of their troops. Many become Eagle Scouts. This is not a popularity contest. Being chosen by your fellow scouts shows they have faith in your leadership abilities. I will now call out the names of the scouts selected for tonight's secret ceremony. Only members of the Order of the Silver Bow and our new candidates may attend."

I was working in the kitchen scrubbing pots, as usual. Eric and James had stuck me with the worst job in the kitchen since the beginning of summer, but I didn't mind. I'd had worse jobs. I was busy scrubbing. The announcements in the dining hall were background noise to me.

"They called your name Dan. You got picked," Eric cried out.

I held a high-pressure spray nozzle in one hand and a large steel pot in the other, unsure of what Eric was talking about.

"Picked for what? I haven't finished cleaning."

"They chose you for the Order of the Silver Bow. You need to get out there."

"Order of the Silver Bow?"

James, Tony, Bruce, and Kurt gathered around me. "Mr. Donaldson called your name," James said.

"Line up at the fireplace," Bruce said, wiping his hands on his damp, full-length apron.

I looked at mom. She smiled and nodded. I untied my apron as I walked through the kitchen, tossed it in the dirty clothes bin, then pushed through the swinging door and walked down the aisle past rows of tables full of scouts. At the front of the hall stood a line of eight candidates. I was happy to see Mark was one of them. I wiped my hand on my pants, then shook each boy's hand before lining up with them.

"Young men, you have the rare honor of being selected as candidates for the Order of the Silver Bow. If you accept, you are to meet at the flagpole on the assembly grounds at nine p.m. Bring a sleeping bag, nothing else. Remember, everything you learn about the Order of the Silver Bow is secret. You can tell no one anything about what happens tonight. You are all dismissed."

Chapter Twenty-One

Nine boys gathered around the flagpole on a moonless summer night. Nine adult leaders stood silently before us, holding flaming torches. One by one, an adult stepped to a boy, tapped him on the shoulder, then led him down a dark trail deep into the woods.

A man with a grim face dimly lit by his torch tapped my shoulder, turned, and walked into the forest. The torch's flickering flame was bright enough for the leader to make out the trail, but the moonless night and thick canopy of old-growth trees created a blanket of darkness that draped over me. After a few minutes leading me deep into the black night, the leader stopped. "Face your fears to find your way back," he whispered, and left me standing alone in the pitch-black forest.

I shivered in the cool chill of night. It's scary, being alone in the dark. Listening when there is no sound, looking where there is no light, I felt the trail through the soles of my tennis shoes sensing the heavy presence of giant trees surrounding me. I feared the dark, where unseen dangers lurked beyond my grasp, ready to attack.

Stepping through the still void, thoughts of the life I had left behind came to mind. My broken home, the constant fighting with my brother, anxiety caused by my mother's yelling, our crappy house. I came to camp believing I could leave behind all the things that sucked in my life. Now, a hundred miles from home, I felt the burdens of that life engulf me. There was no escape.

The dark forest closed in on me like walls of terror, forcing me to confront my demons. Emotions I had hidden away, fears I refused to

139

confront, were the walls I'd erected. The desperate emptiness of my father's abandonment, my mother's disgrace, the shame of our crappy house, the teasing and humiliation of kids at school, feeling helpless and small, believing I was less than others. Freedom meant accepting my life without hiding, releasing the fear of what others thought of me, giving up the false image I presented to the world. Unmasked. The exhausting facade, created to show the best of me, fell away, revealing a boy frightened and alone. I stood trapped in my black box of terror.

I pushed forward, trying to break through the thick walls. Frightened, afraid of what I would face, I gathered my courage, acknowledging my fears step by cautious step. With great effort I inched forward through the black void, cataloging my faults, accepting myself as I am, until I pushed through my walls of terror, leaving fear in the forest like a snake sheds dry skin.

Standing alone, breathing in the cool crisp air, I felt the horrors that possessed me slip away. I stood in the dark, emotionally empty, absorbing the calm of precious peace.

After breaking through those fearsome walls, the tension that wound through me like a spring uncoiled. I welcomed the cool breeze as a soothing tonic. I relaxed. Eric would be proud of me.

Sometimes it takes a walk-through darkness to see yourself in the light. A solitary moment of peace and the strength to accept yourself, not allowing all the crap that happens in your life, define who you are. Accepting your misfortunes and moving on makes you who you become.

I pushed through the trees, stepping into the grassy assembly area where a single adult holding a torch and eight boys waited. When I walked to the group, one boy whispered, "What took you so long?"

The adult leader turned and led us back into the dark wood. The trail grew narrow, forcing us to shuffle along in single file. I walked in total blackness, reaching out to feel my way through the darkness, listening to footsteps, touching the back of the boy ahead of me, just as the boy behind me did to keep our place in line, listening to whispers in the dark.

"I can't see my hand in front of my face." "This is spooky." "Where is he taking us?" I thought this must be what it's like to be blind. I didn't know the boy in front of me. He was a camper, and I couldn't see who walked behind me. When we walked into the forest, Mark was near the end of the line.

When the trail turned sharply, I heard stumbling and movement, a reordering in the line behind me. As we walked deeper into the forest, I became accustomed to my blindness and as we continued; I allowed the now familiar darkness to calm me.

As we trudged along the dark trail, I felt fingers reaching out from behind me like wanting tentacles, seeking, urging to touch. Searching fingers touched the tips of mine tentatively, exploring. The tender touches triggered fleeting sensations, electric tingling, then the fingers retreated, the sensuous energy leaving with them.

The cautious touch reaching through the darkness was tantalizing, yet foreign. My mother never hugged me. She sought affection in other ways. I realized how rare it was that I touched another human except for when I punched my brother; that didn't count. This unexpected contact, the energy from atoms interacting, electrons bouncing off each other, signaling synapses and neurons... was new.

I hadn't expected the touch, but missed the feeling once the fingers left mine. Strange as it was, I thought nothing odd about it. I'd been reaching out in the darkness, touching the back of the boy ahead of me as we slinked along the trail.

It was scary dark. Maybe the other boy had not faced his fears when he stood alone in the forest and reached out now, hoping to calm his lonely soul by making contact with another.

Once again, the fingers sought my touch. This time, after unspoken acceptance, the fingers clawed into mine, searching for my hand. I allowed our fingers to interlock. Without knowing whom I held, I felt the warm sensation of another's touch. I breathed deeply, absorbing the odd feeling of holding another human in my hand.

The trail broadened. Whoever he was, he now walked beside me, joined with me. I peered into the black darkness inches from the other boy's face, but I saw nothing. The hand griped mine tighter, as if begging a question, as we walked through the ancient forest near the western shore of Siltcoos lake. I gave a reassuring squeeze in response. To this day, I do not know who that was.

The trail turned away from the lake and up an incline toward the center of the peninsula, where dark green moss drips off the bark of old giant trees. I stumbled over a thick root and lost my grip on the hand. Boys behind me cried out as others tripped on the root. Some boys fell and others passed them as they stumbled in the dark, shuffling the line once again. I looked up the trail and saw the distant glow of a campfire. The sound of drums and haunting chants reverberated through the trees as we walked up the hill to the fire.

The scout leader stopped us at the edge of a circular clearing with a roaring fire in the center. It surprised me to see that Mark now stood behind me.

A thin boy, wearing only a loincloth and an Indian headdress, his face smeared with red paint, led us to the fire. Nine of us stood around the fire facing an older boy, also in loin cloth wearing a chieftains' headdress, his face and chest streaked with fierce war paint. Dancing flames illuminated the smooth skin of the Indian chief's torso, glistening from the heat of the fire. Two other boys dressed as Indians sat behind the chief at the edge of the clearing, beating drums and chanting.

We were told to place our sleeping bags on the ground behind us. The drum's pounding rhythms and the mesmerizing Indian chant continued as we stood wondering what was about to happen.

The music stopped. All was silent except for the crackling fire. The chief stepped forward, looking hauntingly through the flames at the boys arranged before him. Opening his arms wide, he asked, "Who do you bring to my fire?"

The scout leader took a step forward. "I bring you nine, sent by their brethren. They have braved their fears through darkness, seeking the light of your fire. Nine boys bound for manhood, future leaders of men stand before you, prepared to learn the way of the Silver Bow."

The chief grunted acceptance. The drums beat softly as he spoke. "Long ago, our people suffered hardship from war and famine. Our warriors left the village to wage war and young men went to hunt, never to return. The women, children, and sickly old men wandered barren lands seeking food.

"One day, a young boy left the village walking alone into the wilderness. After many days' journey, thirsty, tired, and hungry, he crawled to the top of a mountain. When he looked to the other side, he saw lush forests and a river flowing through green meadows. As night fell, he marveled at the bright sliver of the silver moon. The next morning, the boy carved a bow from a birch bough in the shape of the silver moon.

"The boy hunted game with the bow, drank from the river, and ate berries as he climbed the mountain. After many days, he delivered his bounty to the people of his village, then led the sickly men, women, and children to the land of plenty. The boy and the silver bow, symbolic of his leadership, saved his people. Few have had the courage to take up the bow, yet I find you at my fire. Give me your pledge now to accept the trials of the order of the silver bow."

The Scoutmaster turned to the nine of us. "Repeat after me. I give my pledge."

We nine spoke in unison. "I give my pledge."

"To accept the silver bow."

"To accept the silver bow."

"And walk the path of leadership, shining like the silver moon as an example to others with honor and righteousness. I do swear." The repeated words reverberated through the trees, echoing into the dark night.

The chief now held a silver bow. He dipped an arrow into the fire, then aimed the flaming tip to the sky, pulling the drawstring to his cheek. He let loose the fiery bolt, sending the flaming arrow in a long arc over the lake as a beacon through the heavens. The drums beat louder.

The chief grunted again, and the drums stopped.

"The boy slept alone in the wilderness, testing his bravery as he sought hope for his people. To honor your pledge, you will sleep alone in the forest this night."

The drums began a low, slow beat. "Pick up your sleeping bags and follow me," the scout leader said, then he led us down a narrow trail into the dark forest. The Indian boy with the small headdress followed.

I heard the rustling of bushes behind me, followed by hushed whispers as I walked along the dark trail, but the shove I received from the Indian boy still shocked me. His violent push off the trail sent me into a thicket of branches followed by his raspy voice admonishing, "Don't move. Sleep where you land."

143

The thicket partially suspended my body. I could not sleep where I had fallen. As I wrestled with the branches, struggling to get free of the bush, I heard someone fall on the other side of the trail, followed by the raspy whispering voice. Then further up the trail, more sounds of the Indian boy pushing other boys from the trail telling them to sleep where they land.

As the trail and forest grew quiet, I moved to my knees and worked to clear an area large enough to sleep when I heard someone crawling toward me. "Who's there?" I whispered.

"It's me. What are you doing?" asked Mark.

"Trying to make a spot big enough to sleep. I got thrown into a bush."

"Come over to my spot. It's all soft pine needles."

"I'm supposed to sleep where I fell."

"I know, but you can't sleep in a shrub, can you?"

"But the silver bow. I made a pledge."

"Shush. I did too. To lead people. I'm leading you out of a thicket to soft pine needles. Besides, you need a good night's sleep. We swim in the morning. Grab your sleeping bag and get over here."

I pulled myself free of the branches and crawled across the trail, unrolling my bag next to Mark's. I hate wearing clothes in a sleeping bag, so I pulled off my shoes, pants, and t-shirt. I tucked my shoes under the head of my bag, then rolled up my pants and shirt, placing them over my shoes as a makeshift pillow.

"Isn't this better?" Mark whispered.

I replied in hushed tones. "Yeah. No sticks poking me in the butt."

"Told you it was better, unless you like getting poked in the butt." I punched Mark's arm. He laughed.

I laid on my back looking up at the tree canopy, hoping to see stars, but the trees were too thick. "How will we wake up for the swim?"

"Sunrise is at five thirty. The sun will wake us up," Mark said, rolling on his side to face me.

"I'll try not to beat you too much," I said.

Mark put his arm across my chest, squeezing me. "First you talk about getting poked in the butt, now you say you're going to beat me. Wow."

"Knock it off. You know what I mean."

"Now that I know how fast you can swim; I won't let you off so easy."

Mark relaxed his arm, but his warm hand rested heavily on my chest.

"Brian said I'll swim faster with the Speedo."

"You will. I'll have to swim even faster to win."

"You might still beat me," I said laying my hand on his.

"Yeah, you wish."

The next morning, I laid awake with my back turned to Mark, staring at bright beams of sunlight piercing the forest canopy, spotlighting ferns, and bushes on the forest floor, leaving other areas in morning shadows. A strange feeling clouded my head. I don't know what I was thinking, but I felt a heaviness bearing down on me. Maybe I was anxious about the swim. That morning, I would achieve the goal I'd strived for the entire summer. What would happen after the swim? Would I still have a purpose, a reason to be on the waterfront?

I heard Mark unzip his bag. "Hey, sun's up. Let's get moving."

We gathered our sleeping bags in our arms, not taking the time to roll them up, and walked past boys sleeping on the trail. We went along that path, then turned down another trail that led us to the staff cabins.

"Did you sleep all right?" Mark asked. I pulled the loose sleeping bag tighter to my chest but didn't respond.

Mark spied me uneasily. "The pine needles were soft. I slept like a baby."

I walked trancelike, feeling gloomy.

We walked without speaking for several minutes. After a time, Mark looked at me questioningly. I glanced back at him with sleepy eyes, then looked away.

As we walked into staff camp, I split off, moving to my cabin.

Mark paused, then said, "I'll grab my stuff and see you at the Waterfront." Again, I didn't respond.

Mark stood watching me walk away. "Don't forget your Speedo. You're gonna need it," then he turned and walked to his cabin.

Chapter Twenty-Two

I wasn't in a good mood, but the mile swim was important. This is what I'd trained for all summer. I couldn't miss it, so I pulled on the red speedo for the first time that morning. It fit tight, hugging my skin. The nylon felt silky smooth. I was ready to swim.

Twenty young scouts and four adult leaders stood on the sandy beach waiting for the swim event to start. Brian was on the dock with Tim and Mark next to him. "Is everyone here? It's time we get this thing started," Brian asked as he mentally counted the swimmers.

I sauntered down the hill and onto the sand carrying my backpack, standing apart from the other boys. It was a cool gray morning. Fog hung over the water, clouding the hills across the lake.

"It's about time you got here. I was about to start without you." Brian noticed I was wearing my baggy red waterfront shorts. "Where's the Speedo I gave you? Don't tell me you lost it." Brian looked at one of the adult leaders. "Teenagers. They'd forget their head if it wasn't screwed on."

I dropped my backpack and stripped off the baggy shorts, revealing the bright red racing suit.

Mark smiled at me, but I didn't acknowledge him.

Brian nodded. "All right. Attention everyone. Welcome to jamboree week's mile swim event. If you look out at the lake, you'll see three buoys marking the course. They might look like empty Clorox bottles, but today they are swim buoys. Swim around each one, keeping the buoy on your right, and return to the beach to complete the swim and earn your mile swim badge. Mark is our pace swimmer. He will not earn a badge. He's got a drawer full of 'em. Some of you will want to race. That's fine, you can chase Mark, but this is not a race, it's a mile swim. We want you to finish. Tim and I will be in the speedboat monitoring the swimmers. Dennis and Rusty will provide support in a rowboat and adult leaders, you will also be in row boats. Come over and get in your boats. I need one of you to take up the rear, following the slowest swimmer. If any swimmer needs help, just wave your hand and someone will be there."

Dennis and Rusty assisted the adult leaders into two rowboats before they moved to their own boat.

"Everybody ready?" Brian asked the swimmers. He raised a whistle to his mouth and blew a long shrill signal to start.

The swimmers ran into the water, falling forward when they got hip deep and began swimming. Mark walked along the dock, watching the scouts swim. I entered the water swimming wide of the group to avoid the crowd of boys, some swimming over other boys.

The Speedo fit skintight, allowing me to glide through the water. I never realized how much drag the baggy shorts created. The speedo set me free. I reached out, pulled, and kicked, slipping gracefully through the water. I breathed on both sides; with each alternating breath, I saw Mark walking on the dock, watching. As the faster swimmers passed the end of the dock, he dove in and quickly overtook them to set the pace.

I lifted my head to spot the first buoy every fourth stroke, just the way Mark had taught me. I stayed wide of the main body of swimmers and aimed for three boys who were trying to catch Mark. Each time I lifted my head to spot the buoy, I was closer to the three boys and aiming for the floating bleach bottles.

That morning, the water felt crisp and tasted sweet. I felt powerful in the red racing suit, skimming through the water. As the pack of three boys rounded the first buoy, I swam past them. Kicking hard, the boys fell farther behind. Swimming with powerful strokes, my right arm bent and my elbow high, fingertips tickling the water as my hand passed close to my ear. I reached out, stretching my body to grab a fistful of water. Pulling my hand along my body, forcing my hips and shoulders to rotate, kicking, and breathing, I lifted my left elbow, ready for the next stroke.

I'd swam almost every afternoon for the past month. My body was a well-trained machine moving in constant smooth motions. I lifted my head and sighted Mark.

He was approaching the second buoy. I pulled harder, chasing him. He must have seen me as he swam around the floating bottles because he sped up. I kicked harder and pulled faster. We'd now left the other swimmers far behind. It was a two-man race across the lake. I exhaled surging bubbles in the water, then gasped in a fresh lung full of air before my body turned, taking two strokes before breathing on the other side, my body cutting a narrow path through the water.

The sun began burning the fog away, with bursts of light cutting through the morning gloom. The third buoy was ahead. Dark green reeds grew tall along the shore and out into the shallow water on this side of the lake. The speedboat idled near the buoy, its engine coughing blue puffs of smoke. Brian and Tim stood in the boat watching the swimmers approach. I swam for Mark and was closing the distance. At this rate, I would catch him just before he swam around the buoy.

I caught images of the buoy and speedboat with each fourth stroke as I raised my head to sight. Dennis and Rusty were rowing, cutting across the swim course, and moving toward the buoy.

Brian must have thought the speedboat was drifting too close to the buoy. He moved to the captain's chair and inched the throttle forward. The engine stalled, choking out a cloud of purple smoke. On my next sighting, Tim had the engine cowling off looking for the problem while Brian hovered angrily over him. Mark swam to the speedboat as it drifted away from the buoy.

I swam past the buoy, but instead of turning toward the shore, swimming to the finish line, I turned back and swam to Mark.

"I thought you fixed the engine. What happened?" Mark asked, treading water at the rear of the speedboat.

"It's been running great. I think Brian flooded it," Tim said, checking the carburetor.

Mark grabbed a long green reed floating in the water and tossed it aside. "Maybe the prop got caught in the weeds. Hang on," Mark said, then dove.

I reached the speedboat while Mark was underwater. Torn pieces of green and yellow reeds and lake grass floated to the surface around me as I treaded water. "Weeds? Is it that shallow here?" I asked.

Mark surfaced. "I got most of it clear. Try starting it now."

"Brian, give it a try." Tim called out.

"Here goes," Brian shouted.

Mark noticed me. "Keep swimming. Don't let this mess you up."

"I'll wait for you. I want to beat you fair and square," I said.

"Now he talks."

The engine cranked slowly but didn't start. We heard Brian cursing.

"Hold on," Mark yelled, then dove again.

I watched as the lead swimmers went around the buoy and swam for shore.

Mark surfaced with a hand full of weeds. "Try it again," he shouted.

I looked anxiously at Mark. "Sorry, about this morning, I was–."

"No need to talk about it. I wake up cranky sometimes too," Mark said over the sound of the engine chugging, struggling to start.

Dennis and Rusty arrived in their rowboat. Dennis was in the bow. Rusty rowed, letting the boat glide close to the rear of the speedboat.

Rusty leaned forward, studying the outboard motor. "I hope we don't have to pull the speedboat in. I'm not as strong as Mark."

"This is proof that Tim sucks as a mechanic," Dennis teased.

"Screw you Dennis," Tim snarled.

The rowboat floated closer, pushing Mark and me to the speedboat. I felt cramped, my head bobbing at water level with the hulls of two boats looming over me. "Rusty, move back. We need some room here," I called out.

Brian shouted. "Rusty, you guys get back on the swim course. We've got this under control."

Mark dove into the weeds a third time.

"We're escorting these guys," Dennis said as Rusty pulled on the oars, moving the boat away from us.

The engine came to life with a plume of blue smoke and violent churning of water.

"Stop. Wait. Mark's down there." I screamed.

Tim fell, looking confused, hugging the engine as the speedboat jerked forward.

The frothy white bubbles turned red.

"Stop, stop." Dennis yelled.

Brian killed the engine as the speedboat floated away.

Mark surfaced with a strange look on his face, holding a handful of weeds. He looked at me with glassy eyes. "I think I got them all," he mumbled. His hand relaxed, letting the weeds drift in the red water.

"Mark, you're hurt," I cried.

"My leg feels weird."

I looked at Dennis. "Help me get Mark out. He's hurt."

"Don't worry about me, runt," Mark stuttered.

Using the lifeguard skills I'd learned, I placed my arm across Mark's chest, allowing his body to rest on my hip as I side-stroked to the rowboat. The cross-chest carry put Mark and me cheek to cheek. My voice trembled as I spoke. "I've got you. We'll get you out. Get you to a doctor."

Mark's body rested heavily on me. The blooded water followed us as I swam. His lips quivered as he whispered, "Remember my promise, whenever you're in the water, I am with… you." Mark's eyes closed.

The rowboat hovered over us. "Dennis, get a hold of Mark's arms. Pull him out," I cried.

Dennis got on his knees, reaching down from the side of the rowboat. He got ahold of Mark's hands and tried to lift the limp body by standing up. As the boat keeled over, Rusty slid to the other side of the boat to balance the weight.

Dennis lost his grip, and Mark's pale body plunged under the surface.

I dove, kicking hard to reach the lifeless boy descending into the deep. Swimming down, I followed angled beams of sunlight penetrating the clear green water, illuminating Mark's youthful face. His long mane of hair floated, swirling in the water like Medusa's snakes.

I heard the whining buzz of an outboard engine overhead as I turned his body, reaching my arm around his chest again, and kicked. When we surfaced, the speedboat was pulling up.

Brian cut the engine and rushed to the side of the boat.

I swam to the speedboat holding Mark. He coughed out water. "Finish it. Swim." He coughed again, then wheezed the words, "I made you a swimmer. Swim,"

I kicked, holding Mark's body so Tim and Brian could reach down and pull him from the lake. Mark gazed at me with stony eyes. "I am one with the water..."

"And the water is one with you," I blubbered, with tears running down my face.

"I'll be with you always," he exhaled the words as the life in his eyes faded, his face relaxed.

As Brian and Tim lifted Mark's ashen body out of the water, I saw his left leg was nearly severed below the knee. No blood flowed. His lower leg, attached by a thin strip of flesh and tendon, dangled, thumping against the boat as they pulled him in.

Brian returned to the side of the boat, looking tearful. "You heard him. Swim. Finish the mile. Finish it for Mark."

No one can see your tears when you swim. I put my head down and kicked, but I barely moved. After a few strokes, I stopped and screamed. I wailed. My cries echoing back to me from the shore. My body released an anguished cry. Dennis and Rusty's boat floated beside me. "Swim, Dan. You gotta swim," Dennis said through tears.

"Do it for Mark," Rusty cried, pulling on his oars.

I took a deep breath, gathered my strength, and swam.

I directed my pain into strength, pulling and kicking harder than I'd ever kicked before, my hips shifting from side to side, cutting through the water. I swam as if an unseen force propelled me. It felt as if I were flying; the water streaming past my body without resistance. Fear had no hold on me. I could have swum through a school of boy biting sturgeon, a swarm of electric eels or a thousand leeches, and nothing would have bothered me. Mark was with me. I felt him watching over me, protecting me.

I swam to shore, crawled onto the sand, and laid there weeping. After my tears ran dry, I sat silently gazing at the lake. As I sat, lost in meditation, a boy appeared above me. He stared at me for a moment, then bent down and placed a mile swim badge in my hand.

I looked at the round white embroidered badge, examining the threads of its blue border and the words MILE SWIM along the top, a seahorse in the center and the letters BSA along the bottom, stitched in red. I stared at that badge, examining every thread that represented the achievement of my summer. A goal attained, but at a cost I could never repay.

Chapter Twenty-Three

I remember little of the summer after the day Mark died. I was lost. Devastated. I stumbled around as if I had died with him. He had saved my life only to die from a freak accident, and I was helpless to save him. I learned later that Brian motored the speedboat to Dunes City, where an ambulance met them at the dock, but it was too late. Mark was gone.

I spent most of the last two weeks of camp in my cabin sleeping. People said their kind words and tried to comfort me, but what words can bring back life? Dennis got one of the older guys to buy a new porn movie at a shop in town, but I wasn't in the mood. Mom said I needed to stay busy, but gave me light duty. I couldn't bear to see the waterfront.

Brian, the waterfront crew, and I grieved in our own ways. I guess that's the way it works.

For me, the only real friend I ever had was gone, and I missed him. I cried for Mark. I cried for myself. I cried for the life he could have lived. A lawyer helping young boys working through the struggles we had endured. Mark would have made a difference. He could have had a wife and children of his own. He would have saved lives. I know he saved mine. I cried.

The day after I got home, I cleaned my room, then cleaned the kitchen and bathroom. After that I opened all the doors and windows to air out the place while I vacuumed the entire house. I don't know what got into me. Maybe after working in the kitchen, I was used to cleaning. Once I got started, I couldn't stop.

I cleaned the garage, sprayed it down with a hose and let it air dry, then I mowed the lawn and picked the weeds. By the time I got to bathing the dogs, Billy joined in and helped. We worked together and didn't fight. Maybe he was growing up.

You should have seen mom's face light up when she came home from work that day.

"I can't believe you boys did all this."

Billy stepped to mom. "Danny did most of the work, but I helped."

"My boys are becoming men." Mom sidestepped Billy and hugged me, then kissed my cheek. It was just a peck, but she'd never done that before. It felt nice. The soft touch of her lips lingered there for minutes.

I hadn't seen her that happy in years. It was like I had lifted a tremendous burden from her. She was instantly lighter and at ease. Had my cleaning house helped her breakthrough one of her walls of terror?

I realized the challenge of running a household by herself must have overwhelmed her. Feeling defeated, she let the house go, and sought to soothe her terrors, seeking fleeting pleasure, which inevitably created more pain.

"You boys must be hungry. I feel like cooking," she said.

That night we sat at the dining table and ate dinner together with no yelling. It felt like family.

The next afternoon, she took us to River Park. We sat at a picnic table eating takeout fried chicken, then Billy and I played Frisbee. Mom joined for a while, even though she's horrible at Frisbee. She stayed home every night that week.

Everyone has their struggles. I realized mom had to work through her issues just like I had. Cleaning the house didn't solve all her troubles, but maybe I helped lighted her burden just a little.

A week after returning home, I received a check in the mail. My salary for working the summer at Camp Baker. I didn't deposit the check in my savings account right away. I kept it in my room, on top of my dresser, where I could see it.

Looking at the check reminded me of my first day at camp standing in the parking lot, watching my mother speed away. My motivation to get that job was to earn money. Now I had the money and all I did was stare at the check.

I'd thought it would be easy to fit in and make friends, easy as pie. It wasn't so easy. I faced challenges that summer I could not have foreseen, but I learned so much. Creating the façade of a happy, confident Danny Novak, I tried to bury the frightened, insecure boy they called Pigpen, hoping people would like the new me.

I wasn't alone in this. Kurt stayed silent for half the summer, afraid we wouldn't accept him or treat him like a regular guy if we knew he was rich and cultured. Mark struggled, being stereotyped as a bad boy when he wasn't bad at all. He was the best of us.

I learned it was the walls I put up, trying so hard to be liked and accepted, that trapped me in a box of insecurity and self-doubt. That summer I walked through darkness, faced mortality, suffered pain, and broke through the walls I had built.

That September, I would be a freshman at Lebanon High. One afternoon, I was lying on the couch watching the Partridge Family when there was a knock at the door. Billy rushed to see who was there, then shouted, "Danny, it's for you."

When I went to the door, I faced a tall, muscular man with a square jaw and short cropped brown hair. He stood stiffly at our doorstep wearing a red Lebanon High School polo shirt with WARRIORS embroidered on the breast pocket. "Are you Dan Novak?" He asked.

"Yes, sir." I don't know why I added the sir. He looked like a sir.

"I'm coach Haworth. Head coach of the swim team. I got a call from a friend of yours, a fella named Brian. He said I need you on my swim team."

"Brian called?"

"He said you might need a kick in the ass to get you going, but you'd be worth my trouble. Then he said something I didn't understand. He insisted I tell you, don't do jack shit."

I smiled.

"Brian said you'd know what that means. Oh, and Molly says hello. She and the boys are doing fine."

I was in a daze, shocked that Brian would call and even more surprised that the swim coach came to my house.

"Are you going to be worth my trouble, Dan Novak?"

Digging my hand into my pants pocket, I held the mile swim badge, rubbing my thumb across the smooth stitching. "I'll do my best."

"Good. I expect nothing less from my swimmers. We swim tomorrow morning at six a.m. Don't be late and bring your own swim goggles."

"Thanks Coach. I'll be there."

The next morning, I swam wearing my red Speedo.

As soon as I hit the water, I felt Mark with me. While the other kids complained and struggled with the swim sets, swimming set me free.

Mark said, wear it always, and I did. I swam my way through high school and four years on my college swim team wearing a red Speedo every workout, swim meet, and race. When my suit wore out, I bought another red Speedo. During school swim meets, I wore the team swimsuit over my red Speedo. During my adult life, I took up open water swimming, competing in long distance ocean swim events around the world, always wearing my red Speedo.

I never got to say goodbye. As far as I know, there was never a funeral. I've searched and there's no record of a burial. I like to imagine Mark's father scattered his ashes at sea. Mark would have liked that. Poseidon would have welcomed his son's return.

I often think of Mark's promise. Whenever you're in the water, I am with you. Every time I'm in a pool, a lake, a river, or the ocean, I feel his spirit with me because I know Mark is one with the water and the water is one with him.

As the years passed, I understood that the pains of youth, overcoming grief, struggling to fit in, and growing up in an imperfect family, all added up to something immeasurable. I lived a life with meaning that grew from a life of suffering.

Mark's promise has never left me, and I pray he knows I did my best to honor his last request.

I swim.

The Legend of the Double-bitted Axe Man

A Camp Baker Story by Mike McCoy

During the summer of 1961, when Camp Baker was known as Camp Tsiltcoos, six scouts left for an overnight canoe trip. The boy's never returned.

Scout leaders searched the campsite on the east side of the lake the next day, but there was no sign of the boys. Hopes of finding the missing scouts rose when a boater spotted three canoes on a rocky beach south of Arrowhead Point.

A search led to an old rundown house, hidden in the dark forest, an area off limits to scouts at the end of the peninsula.

When searchers entered the house, they found the bodies of six boys. Their heads chopped off by a double-bitted axe. Even more frightening, their heads were missing.

Inside the house they found a bloody boot print, a blood covered double-bitted axe, and more double-bitted axes next to the fireplace, by the front door, and two in the bedroom. In the kitchen, where the pantry should be, a strange door was open. There was no doorknob, but it had six butterfly latches to secure the door. Someone had made each of the latches and four hinges on the door from double-bitted axe heads. Someone or something had unlocked every latch on the door.

Neither the killer nor the boys' heads were ever found. The story goes that a boy innocently opened the latches that night, releasing a terrible axe wielding beast who removes the head of anyone who trespasses.

After the tragedy, the camp was closed for the summer. Camp management erected a new fence and posted no trespassing signs blocking access to the mysterious house, and in 1963, they changed the name to Camp Baker with a grand celebration.

Every summer, hundreds of scouts visit the camp, swim in the lake, earn merit badges, and run carefree down forest trails, but at night when young scouts gather around their campfires, they are told the story of the mysterious deaths and the legend of the double-bitted axe man.

A dream becomes a nightmare

A beautiful young girl, with dark hair and milk white skin wearing a white lace dress and a red petticoat, steps out of darkness to stand before a large round saw spinning so fast the blade's teeth are a blur. The girl slowly reaches out until her tiny finger touches the whirling blade. She withdraws her hand from the biting saw, staring at a single drop of blood on her fingertip.

The wagon came to a sudden stop, shocking Rolf Birger from his dream. It wasn't the first time he'd dreamt that dream on his long voyage to the state of Oregon. He'd dreamt the same strange vision nearly every night of his travels. Arriving at the small coastal town of Florence in July 1897, Rolf was at the end of a journey that had started months before in Sweden, when he received a letter from his uncle asking the young man to join him to help run his lumbermill.

Rolf had a firm jaw and dark, wavy hair. He was taller than most men, broad-shouldered, and strong as a bull. Rolf had spent his youth in Sweden's forests felling trees and chopping wood. Rolf towered over most men, but still found it odd when he faced another man on a street or walkway that the other man would always step aside, allowing Rolf to pass.

Young Rolf jumped down from the wagon and looked, searching for his uncle, who had planned to meet him. Rolf was disappointed that his uncle wasn't there, but was happy to have reached his destination. He marveled at the burgeoning village with its raised wooden walkways, houses lining the street, and buildings, a bank, a saloon, a general store, and a hotel.

An old Indian chief wearing a feathered headdress stood at the store entrance. Rolf had never seen a real Indian before. He smiled and nodded to the stoic chief as he walked past to inquire inside.

The shopkeeper reported that Rolf's uncle had died under mysterious circumstances a month before and the name of the mill had changed. When Rolf left the store, the old Indian was gone.

The lumbermill sat on the shores of Siltcoos lake six miles south of town. At the mill, Rolf learned his uncle had gained a new partner shortly before his death. Mr. Simon Booth. Mr. Booth, surprised to meet his deceased partner's nephew, greeted Rolf like family, but secretly worried about his claim on the mill.

That evening, Mr. Booth served a large dinner of venison and bear meat with plenty of beer and whiskey to wash it down. The mill owner's three sons were unkept and surly, but his daughter, Beth Anne, was a beauty with black hair and milk white skin. Beth Anne looked a dream. She smiled at Rolf, causing his heart to flutter. Beth left the table when the men poured more whiskey, but whispered in Rolf's ear as she passed him. *Meet me in the mill at mid-night*, she'd said.

Rolf staggered into the dark mill at the appointed hour. He spotted the young beauty wearing a dress of white lace. The mill was dark. Beth Anne, illuminated by the light of a lamp, stood next to a large saw. The blade spun with a metallic whir. Beth Anne extended her finger, beckoning Rolf to come near. As Rolf's hulking figure stepped through the darkness, the mill owner's sons fell upon him, swinging double-bitted axes.

Rolf did his best to fight them off, tossing the men aside, but they came back swinging. The sharp blades of the double-bitted axes cut deep into Rolf's flesh. Mortally wounded, the strong young man fell hard to the floor. The drunken sons, exhausted from the furious fight of blade and blood, stumbled off, leaving Rolf for dead.

Before darkness turned to dawn, the old Indian crept slowly into the dark mill. He found Rolf, barely alive, lying-in blood, and dirt. With great effort, he pulled Rolf's massive bulk to the lake and rolled his body into a canoe, then paddled silently across the still waters to skeleton island, a place white men dared not go.

The old Indian mixed poultices to treat Rolf's wounds. As the old man labored over Rolf's injuries, he spoke. "Your uncle was a good man, honest and fair. He called me Joe, Indian Joe and let me work in the mill, like other men. Mr. Booth is an evil man. He cheated your uncle. Booth sent me and the other workers away, hired his own men and turned them against your uncle."

Old Joe turned mud mixed with herbs in his hands, then pressed the healing mud into a deep cut on Rolf's leg. He spoke again to the listless form, lit by the flames of a small fire. "Now I stand at the general store everyday begging for scraps." Indian Joe mixed a tea, but Rolf would not drink.

Two suns and two moons passed, but Rolf did not stir. Late that night, as a last hope to revive the young man, Joe took a red glowing coal from the fire. Chanting sacred words over it, blowing on the coal to keep it alive, he placed the glowing orb into a deep wound in Rolf's chest. As the burning ember sunk into his chest, Rolf's body jerked alive with fire burning in his eyes.

Over the next weeks, Rolf's body healed, but visions of double-bitted axes thrashing his body tormented his mind. One night, Rolf paddled across the lake to the mill. He crept into the mill owner's house and, using a double-bitted axe, chopped off the heads of Mr. Booth, Beth Anne, and Booth's three sons while they slept.

Rolf paddled to the end of a long peninsula near the island, land he inherited from his uncle. Carrying a large burlap sack, he walked up a slope until he entered a large clearing. There, he buried the heads in the shape of a 'V,' placing the head of Simon Booth at the apex. Rolf then planted a sapling over each head.

Indian Joe guarded over the Rolf, attempting to ease the rage that burned in his soul. Rolf's body healed, but his mind forever bedeviled with images of the axe turned Rolf from a man into a savage beast, removing the head of anyone who dared step foot on Skelton Island.

After a time, Joe moved the beast to the uncle's house at the end of the long peninsula overlooking Siltcoos lake. Joe converted the pantry into a room secured with reinforced hinges made from double-bitted axe heads and six locks to hold the beast. The quiet darkness calmed the rage that fueled the monster.

Years went by. Indian Joe died, but the coal burned red hot in the beast's heart, locked away in his dark tomb.

Before he died, Joe built a fence across the end of the peninsula and posted signs warning others not to trespass.

After the deaths of the six scouts, everything was normal until the summer of 1968.

That summer, four boys who heard the legend of the double-bitted axe man were determined to learn if the story was true.

The next day, the four young scouts dared each other to find the axe man's house and spend the night in it. With overnight packs, they hiked late that afternoon to the end of the trail, challenging themselves to be brave enough to stay in the house if they found it.

When the trail ended, they pushed through dense overgrown bushes until they entered a dark dead forest where retched trees bled sticky pitch and dead wood covered ground. Dry branches broke under the boy's feet as they walked. They tread deeper into that dark grove until they reached a wooden fence covered with signs warning them not to trespass.

The boys climbed the fence, then scurried to a low hedge. Beyond the hedgerow, in the center of the dark clearing, they discovered a dull, weathered old house. Black mold grew on the wood siding. Green moss-covered the wood shingled roof. The house had a broad porch along the front and a large picture window covered with dreary, heavy drapes.

"The house is real," a boy gasped.

"It looks abandoned," said a second boy.

"Let's get closer," said the third boy.

"You want to go in there?" asked the first boy.

"And get chopped by a double bitted-axe," said the second boy.

"Look." the fourth boy shrieked, breathing hard, making the sound, "Ooh, ooh, ooh," pointing at the window.

The boy's eyes locked on the window. Something had pulled a corner of the curtain back.

"Was the curtain like that before?" The first boy asked.

The curtain dropped.

The boys ran screaming through the black forest, branches breaking under their feet like brittle bones. They ran, scared out of their wits, until they came upon a wooden shed.

When they entered the shed, they found a table with an oil lamp, chairs, a small potbellied stove, and bunks stacked three beds high.

Afraid to walk any further through the dark forest, the boys settled in for the night. They lit a fire in the stove, cooked hot dogs, and retold their experience of the scary house hidden in the black forest and the curtain in the window that moved, scaring themselves again, until they grew tired.

When it was time to sleep, the boys drew straws since there were three bunks and four boys. One boy stood holding the shortest stick while the other three laughed, crawling into their beds. With no bed for him, the boy crawled under the lowest bunk and slept on the floor.

The boys talked and teased each other until they drifted off to sleep.

The next morning, the boy who slept on the floor, under the lowest bunk, woke to strange sounds. When he looked out from below the bed, he saw big heavy boots stepping across the floor to the bunk. He then heard three sharp whacks, like the sound of a blade chopping through wet wood. Then a bloody double-bitted axe hit the floor with a heavy thud. The boy, afraid for his life, watched rivulets of blood streak down the silver blade. His fear amplified when blood dripped from the bunk above onto his cheek, but he dared not make a sound.

When the heavy boots moved to the stove at the far end of the shed, the boy scooted out from his hiding place. As he stood, he gasped in fright. He was staring into the dead vacant eyes of his three friends'. Their severed heads lined along the top bunk.

The hulking man dressed in black turned from the stove and reached for his axe.

The boy ran out of the shed with the axe man giving chase, swinging his bloodied blade through the air. Fearing for his life, the boy ran through the forest, leaping over fallen trees, hopscotching through tangled roots like zombie arms grabbing for his feet.

The double-bitted axeman growled and snorted like a beast, running inches behind the boy. Running for his life, his eyes darting over his shoulder, the boy got glances of a fierce bearded man wearing a cloak of black bear fur.

The boy ran up a hill toward the center of the peninsula, where he came upon a circular clearing, a meadow of green grass and trees. He paused, noticing the trees grew in the shape of a "V." The tallest trees at the apex. As the lines extended across the meadow, each tree was shorter and younger than the one before. The boy noticed fresh holes dug at the end of the rows of trees.

A twig snapped, breaking the silence of the meadow. The boy ducked as an axe swung over his head. He ran from the gruesome snarling beast, all the way back to his camp without ever looking back.

No one has died at Camp Baker since the day those three boys lost their heads, but the rumors persist. They say the double-bitted axe man roams the black forest watching for anyone who dares trespass.

Now before you scoff and claim the legend is a made-up story meant to scare young scouts, I'm here to tell you that is not so. I know the legend of the double-bitted axeman is true because — I am that boy. The boy who got away.

About On the Waterfront

I was twelve years old when these stories came to me, the essence of the stories, anyway. I was a scout at Camp Baker staying at the Tyee campsite. One morning, I was having some intestinal issues. I sat in a wooden outhouse on a bluff overlooking Siltcoos lake with the door open, gazing out at the water.

The first story was about two boys swimming the mile swim. An accident occurred and one boy was gravely injured, but before he died, he promised his friend he would always watch over him whenever he swam.

The second story, the Legend of the Double-bitted Axeman, came to me next. I shared this story with my brother and close friends who have told the story to their children over the years.

That was it. They weren't fully thought-out stories, but the ideas rattled around in my mind for the next fifty-plus years. Ever since that day, I thought about becoming a writer and promised myself I would put these stories down on paper one day. It was not a simple task. It's taken years for me to craft these tales.

Every story contains a bit of reality. There really was a house at the end of the peninsula at Camp Baker. I went there with a group of friends, and I can swear the curtain moved, and we ran, scared out of our wits. From that scary moment, I've carried fond memories and created a story I've held close for a lifetime.

On the Waterfront is fiction, but many of the episodes in the story are real. If you asked me if I was Danny or Mark, I would say some of each.

I was a member of staff at Camp Baker for two summers in 1973 and 1974. I worked in the kitchen and on the waterfront. Brian and Molly were real people, although I don't remember if those are their real names. I was happy to be away from home and my bratty little brother. There were some rather gross chores I had at home involving animals, and I worked hard to make and save money.

Working on the waterfront, I swam several mile swims and there was an old green rowboat I loved to row. One day, a storm came up suddenly and a sailboat overturned. The speedboat that went to rescue the sailboat had engine trouble. I rowed out through turbulent water and pulled both boats back to shore through crashing waves in a violent storm. Those and many other story elements really happened. There are many stories behind the story. They say you write what you know. I have done exactly that, drawing deeply from the experiences of my youth and the wonderful times I spent at Camp Baker.

The one real boy in the story is Jeff, the engineer. Jeff Adams did amazing things with sticks and twine. He made gates that would open fifty feet away with a pull on a pinecone. He made crossbows with arrows that flew across camp, and more. His ingenuity amazed me.

One day, while riding in the back seat of a car, an errant bullet fired by Charles Arthur Hein, a prison escapee being chased by the police, hit Jeff in the back of the head.

Jeffery Burton Adams died instantly at sixteen years old. I believe his death was a significant loss to the world. Imagine what that boy would have created if he had lived.

I hope you enjoyed reading On the Waterfront. It's a deeply personal story for me, one that was difficult to get down on paper, but I am happy I have finally fulfilled the boyhood promise I made to myself so long ago.

About the Author

Mike McCoy is an Eagle Scout and a novelist. His debut novel ASTEROIDS–Bridge to Nowhere, received high praise from critics and selected as a semifinalist for the 2020 Publishers Weekly Booklife Prize. Because of the research Mike conducted for the novel, he has been a frequent guest on talk radio shows, including Coast to Coast AM with George Noory discussing the risks to Earth from asteroids.

Mike is also an international businessman and a serial entrepreneur who has traveled extensively. Mike worked in the consumer electronics industry for thirty years. The company he founded developed a variety of innovative products which were sold in retail stores in over forty countries around the world. Many innovations Mike and his company developed were "first in the world" products.

Mike is also an accomplished athlete known for long distance events. He completed a full Ironman Triathlon in 2006. He thought running fifty miles would be a wonderful accomplishment, so for his fiftieth birthday, he ran a double Marathon (52.4 miles). In 2018, Mike celebrated his sixtieth birthday with a six-hundred-mile bike ride from Florence, Oregon, to San Francisco, California.

Somehow, he finds time to write.

<u>Novels</u>
ASTEROIDS – Bridge to Nowhere
TAC Force – Sons of Khan
On the Waterfront

<u>Short Stories</u>
Obsidian – Tales of Karanga

Please remember to leave a review

Check Mike's website for news, updates, and to join his mailing list
www.MikeMcCoy.me

Find Mike on Facebook
www.facebook.com/AuthorMikeMcCoy

Amazon's Author Central
Amazon.com: Mike McCoy: Books, Biography, Blog, Audiobooks, Kindle

More from Mike McCoy

If you enjoyed On the Waterfront, you might enjoy other works written by Mike McCoy.

TAC FORCE—Sons of Khan—Launching 2023

Frank Callahan was the first man to get kicked off the Moon, the first man to hitch a ride back, the first homeless man on the Moon, and the most unlikely hero.

The Grand Luna hotel is about to open at Malapert Station, a thriving base near the South Pole of the Moon. The hotel will create a burgeoning moon-based economy. While helping save a scientist from a life-threatening accident, Frank learns about a metal derived from a unique ore discovered near the base, and The Terrain Alliance Council's (TAC) efforts to keep the discovery secret.

The Sons of Khan invade during the hotel's pre-opening gala and capture everyone at Malapert Station. Everyone but Frank.

Astrid Astana, leader of the Khan, is determined to control the base. The morning after the invasion, a group of workers rebel and the Sons of Khan respond with violent action. When Astrid learns Frank is free, she sends soldiers to hunt him down. To Astrid, Frank is an annoying little man disrupting her plans.

For Frank, it's him against Astrid and the Sons of Khan. He creates confusion, death, and chaos while trying to save the base commander and his friends.

Frank uses his wits, skills, and unique capabilities to fend off the invaders. After Frank rescues his friends, the Sons of Khan retaliate with a devastating attack that threatens to destroy the base. Frank, TAC Force, and the base workers fight to save the Malapert Station and rescue the woman he loves.

While battling the Sons of Khan, Frank learns the true reason for the invasion and is confronted with questions about which side is good, who is bad, and how controlling perceptions and beliefs can be more destructive than bullets.

Sample Chapter: TAC Force – Sons of Khan

Be patient, dear reader, old tales take time to tell.
I recite our tumultuous history under duress.
It is they who demand these stories be told.
You don't know them.
They watch.

I was young and foolish those days, naïve and headstrong. Emotion and desire guided my path, with little thought to planning things out. I had a dream, a strong desire that emboldened me to take a foolhardy adventure.

Two and a half centuries before, when the American frontier was expanding, people said go west, young man. That's what young men did to make their way in the world, seeking fortune or a better life.

My heart said get back to the Moon young man. It was the land of opportunity.

I'd been to the Moon and worked at Malapert Station. As you will learn, Commander Harding, the boss of the base, sent me back to Earth. I was Twenty-six years old and already been kicked me off the Moon. Not many people can say that.

The Moon pulled on the blood in my veins like a rising ocean tide. I'd do anything to get back.

—————

I always hated this part. It's bad enough when you're sitting in a padded chair with a video monitor fourteen inches from your face, watching the clock countdown to launch, waiting for your guts to get yanked to your feet. It's worse when you can't see what's happening.

I knew it was coming, but I didn't know when. I heard rumbling. Everything started shaking. I sat scrunched in a small dark storage cabinet, clutching a backpack, my chin at my knees. Not the best idea I've ever had, but my options were limited.

The sudden shock of the thrusters felt like a swift kick in the ass as the vibration and pressure intensified, pushing my body painfully down against the smooth, hard walls of the cabinet I had secured myself in.

The roaring fury of thirty-five Ravax VX engines deafened me. Their sudden thrust and jarring tremors pounded my body like a heavyweight boxer. The violent thrashing transitioned to oscillating numbness as the Star Cruiser accelerated through the lower atmosphere.

Earth did not want to let go. Its claws pulled at me while the rocket fought against the force of gravity, powering ever upward. My body position—ouch. The pressure forced my nose down past my knees. My back doesn't bend that way. It hurt like hell.

The backpack, the only soft thing in that hard box, was my single comfort. I couldn't breathe. Sweat dripped from my forehead. I felt as though I was being crushed under the weight of an enormous cement block. Hell yes, I was scared. I was afraid I'd black out, or worse.

I'm not a big guy, but I could have died in that dark, cramped box. How disappointing that would have been. All my efforts, months of planning, only to die a crumpled heap in a storage cabinet. As the pressure increased, I concentrated on sipping air into my lungs. My body screamed pain, sounding an alarm that I should not be doing this.

I endured that agony for what felt like an eternity yet lasted only two minutes before the pressure eased off.

This was a momentary pause to reduce stress on the spacecraft's structure while it experienced maximum dynamic pressure, or Max Q.

I knew I had but a momentary reprieve. Quickly, I straightened my vertebrae with very audible cracks and hurriedly gulped air until I felt woozy. The pressure was building. Here it comes, I thought.

The force of the engines rocketing to full thrust squashed me in my box again. The eerie cry of an injured cat screaming outside penetrated the darkness. From experience, I knew it was thin air slipstreaming over the passenger module, but knowledge did not quell fear.

The torturous ascent continued through a series of explosive booster separations, periods of 1g acceleration, during which I attempted to stretch my cramped legs, followed by a final acceleration to 3g that made me feel like I was being crushed in a trash compactor. I prayed the spacecraft wouldn't implode, crumpling like an aluminum can under pressure—which still happened occasionally.

I suffered through the crushing pain, risking my life and freedom to get back, knowing I should not go, but nothing could deter a young man driven by the nagging angst to make something of his life. The desire to succeed, the quest for adventure and dreams of riches.

I flew headlong toward an unimagined destiny, unaware that another person's plans would affect my life and the lives of others. How could I have known an enemy lurked whose goals would test the limits of my being, that their ambition would change everything?

Finally, the thrust stopped. Silence never sounded so sweet. The pressure eased and my pain diminished. It was a wondrous feeling. I bumped my head on the roof of the cabinet as I floated weightless in my box. Oh, the joy of being in space.

I opened the door of my cabinet and drifted out, stretching my arms, legs, and back in the open space of the cargo deck, the lowest level of the six-deck, one-hundred-passenger cruiser.

I grabbed my backpack, also floating in the cabinet, and began changing into a United Launch Systems flight suit I had snagged weeks before. Changing clothes in zero gravity isn't as easy as it sounds. Watching me wriggle into floating pants and pushing off the wall, chasing runaway shoes, would have been comical.

I stuffed my black jumpsuit into the backpack, then pushed the pack into the cabinet. At least I wouldn't look like a loading porter, which is what I was. I'd taken the job loading cargo for freight launches and the infrequent passenger flight to the Moon and Mars four months earlier, right after my return to Earth. It took me months to find a crack in the system that would allow me to sneak my way onto a flight. I had a single goal to satisfy—an overwhelming, undeniable desire. I had to get back to the Moon.

ASTEROIDS—Bridge to Nowhere

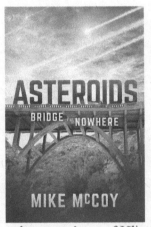

Mike McCoy's highly regarded debut novel can be found on Amazon and everywhere books are sold.

9.5 out of 10–The BookLife prize

Although asteroids hitting Earth is not a new story idea, McCoy brings a fresh approach to his apocalyptic plot. From the futuristic weapons to the artificial atmosphere of New Arcadia to the vampire-like antagonist who gains immortality from the blood of children to two characters' use of Klingon as code, this story is full of unique ideas.

McCoy's combination of everyday language and scientific jargon is extremely well balanced. There isn't a boring passage in the book.

4.3 Stars–IndieReader

ASTEROIDS is an extremely immersive adventure with memorable characters, tons of high-tech flourish and despite being a massive book, debut novelist Mike McCoy keeps things moving briskly.

FIVE Stars–Ashley Causey–Oh Hey! Books

What Clive Cussler does for action/adventure; Mike McCoy does for science fiction. He has captured a fresh perspective on the future. The gamer aspect was timely and exciting. I am anxious to see where Mike McCoy takes us next.

Sample Chapter from ASTEROIDS – Bridge to Nowhere

Chapter 1: Frog Giggin'

Near Future: Briarcliffe Acres—Myrtle Beach, South Carolina USA

Early Sunday Morning

Sander lies in his bed, listening in the dark. Silence. His parents are asleep. He looks to his younger brother's bed across the room. Heavy breathing. Good, the little brat's asleep. Sander checks the time: 1:00 a.m. He needs to get moving. His best friend, Brody, will be down the street.

Sander slides out of bed and pulls on the clothes he'd tossed to the floor earlier. The boy's bedroom features a window at a height of five feet. Sander had removed the window screen a few months earlier and hid it behind the bushes in the backyard.

Sander also moved his old toy box to rest beneath the window, creating a perfect step. Now the window is waist height; easy for him to get out. It's a six-foot jump from the window to the grass, a perfect way to sneak out of the house.

He's snuck out many weekend nights to meet up with Brody and other friends to hang out or go frog giggin' in the South Carolina wetlands. After slipping on his shoes, he steps up on the wooden toy box and slides the window open.

"Where are you going?" The voice of his younger brother, Colton, breaks the night's silence. The sound startles Sander. He's snuck out and back many times without waking Colton.

"Shush. You'll wake up Mom and Dad," Sander says in a hushed tone.

"Going out on a date with your boyfriend, Brody?" asks Colton.

Sander responds to Colton's comment by stepping from the toy box to his brother's bed, then dropping to his knees, straddling his brother's body. He lowers his fist to the center of Colton's chest. "One punch, brat. One hard punch, right here, and your heart will stop beating. You'll be dead. Good riddance!" Sander presses his knuckled fist hard into Colton's chest, knowing it's painful.

Colton thrusts his hips, attempting to buck his brother off, causing the headboard of the bed to knock against the wall with a loud thunk. Both boys freeze. They listen for parents awakened by the noise. Colton whispers, "Let me go with you."

Sander grinds his fist into Colton's chest once more for good measure, before rising and stepping back to the toy box. "Find your own friends, wimp. We don't want you tagging along," argues Sander.

"I won't bother you guys. Come on. Dad said I should get out of the house more," Colton pleads.

"Yeah, he said you should make your own friends, not hang out with mine," Sander replies, as he slides the window open wide enough to scramble through.

"I'll tell Mom you've been sneaking out."

"You tell Mom and I'll kill you, you friggin' little brat. God, why couldn't I have been an only child?"

"Let me go with you and I won't tell."

"All right. Shit! Don't make any noise and stay away from me."

Colton throws back his blankets to reveal he's dressed and ready for adventure. The boys then crawl out the window and jump to the grass.

Sanders' friend Brody waits down the street. Brody is a fifteen-year-old boy, tall and thin, with unruly dark hair and a face full of acne.

Brody spots the boys approaching. "Hey, Sander. I almost gave up on ya. What? You brought the little Colt? I thought he's afraid of the dark."

"He begged me to bring him along."

"Hey, Colt. Better watch out, the swamp monster might get you!"

"Yeah, let's feed him to the swamp monster, or dump him into the pond and frog gig him," exclaims Sander as the three boys walk along the street, heading toward the wetlands of scattered ponds and tall grass.

"Ah, knock it off, guys," Colton replies. "I'm not afraid. In the wetlands, it's the coyotes you need to worry about. Didn't you hear on the news? They found two teenagers in the wetlands last week. Their bodies all chewed up by coyotes. It was a bloody mess."

"Coyotes! We've never seen coyotes out here, have we, Sander?" Brody asks.

"Nah, Colton's making it up. I don't think we have coyotes on the Carolina coast," Sander says.

The boys walk along a dirt trail that winds through tall grass leading into the wetlands. "If you listen, you might hear a coyote howl in the distance," Colton whispers in his creepiest voice.

"Shut up, Colton! You won't scare us," Sander says, as he picks up his pace to walk abreast of Brody. Colton walks behind the older boys, then pulls his shirt over his mouth and lets out a soft howl, trying to make it sound like the howl is coming from a distance.

"Colton, knock it off. I know that was you. I should have tied you to your bed and gagged you, so you can't squeal to Mom." Then Sander hears another howl. He's startled and stops for a moment to listen.

Brody tries to keep his composure, but when Sander looks at him, he can't contain himself and breaks into a giggle. Colton howls again. Sander smiles, then makes a loud exaggerated howl. The boys walk through the wetlands howling in the night.

After several howls, the boys walk through the thicket of trees that ring their favorite frog gigging pond where the sound of croaking frogs replaces the sound of howling boys. Brody goes to a nearby tree to retrieve the frog gigging sticks he and Sander had prepared earlier. They'd cut long thin branches, stripped them of leaves, and sharpened one end to make six-foot-long spears. Brody hands a spear to Sander.

"We only have two spears, so you have to watch our deadly attacks," Sander says to Colton as he holds his spear like a warrior.

Colton doesn't look disappointed.

"Don't worry. If I get tired, I'll let you use my spear," says Brody.

Sander walks through the tall grass to the edge of the pond, holding his spear at the ready. He listens and looks for nearby frogs, then jabs his spear into the weeds at the pond's edge, making a sound. "Hi-ya!" He extracts the spear from the weeds. No frog.

Brody tiptoes along the edge of the pond, looking for a good spot to mount his attack. He steps closer to the edge. Water seeps into his shoes. He sees a frog, raises his spear, and thrusts. The frog jumps just in time to miss certain skewering. "Damn it! I missed," cries Brody. Sander and Brody search for their next quarry.

Colton quickly loses interest in the frog-spearing expedition. He studies the sky. It's a clear moonless night, allowing the stars to shine brighter. He can make out some constellations he learned about at scout camp. As he gazes at the stars, a bright light appears in the eastern sky over the Atlantic. Growing bigger and brighter, the light moves fast toward the shore, heading directly over wetlands.

"Hey guys, look at the sky," Colton yells. "It's a shooting star."

Brody and Sander look up, spears in hand. The object becomes blindingly bright before it explodes in the sky. The boys cover their eyes, shielding them from the sudden brightness. They see the explosion first. The sound comes later.

Brody jumps and hollers, "Wow, did you see that? It blew up!"

"Dang, that was awesome! Maybe it's an alien spaceship crashing to Earth," exclaims Sander.

Seconds after the explosion, a strange sphit, sphit, sphit sound races past the boys, sending ripples across the calm pond, tearing leaves off trees, and causing some branches to fall. The boys stand quiet and still. A dog barks in the distance.

Twenty seconds after the explosion, a tremendous hot wind knocks the boys over. The wind passes and all is calm. Sander attempts to stand. He gets up on one knee.

Colton, laying in the mud, looks to his brother and sees several blood spots staining Sander's shirt. "You're bleeding."

Sander looks at his shirt and notices the blood spots. "I don't feel anything." Sander looks at Colton. Colton has several spots of blood on his shirt, and they're growing larger.

"You're the one bleeding, don't blame me." Sander looks over to Brody, who's lying in the mud. He isn't moving.

Colton struggles to move. He tries to get out of the muddy patch he fell in, but he can't move his body. He whimpers, "I'm telling Mom." Those are Colton's last words. He lies quiet and still at the muddy edge of the pond. The blood spots on his shirt swell, growing into one big blood stain.

Sander feels warm blood run over his night-chilled skin. The blood is his. He tries again to stand. With great effort, he gets to his feet and stumbles over to Brody. In the dim light, he can see Brody's face. There's a black hole where his friend's nose was. Brody is dead.

Sander turns and takes a few steps up the trail, then slumps to his knees before toppling over onto his side. He lies on the muddy trail breathing in halting gasps. He doesn't move or cry out. Sander's eyes are open. He observes the wetland grass and watches a small bug climb up a stalk. "Damn, I left the bedroom window open." He exhales. Sander is dead.

CTBTO Monitoring Station

The Comprehensive Nuclear-Test-Ban Treaty Organization (CTBTO) has a network of forty-five infrasound stations designed to track atomic blasts across the planet. The strange thing is, beginning in the year 2000, they intercepted strange sounds that were not atmospheric atomic blasts. Through the year 2030, the infrasound system had catalogued one hundred eighty-six major explosions on Earth. A-bombs didn't cause any of the explosions. They were all the result of asteroid strikes.

The CTBTO dug into the reports. The asteroid events ranged in energy from one to six hundred kilotons. By comparison, the bomb that destroyed the Japanese city of Hiroshima was a fifteen-kiloton device. Fortunately, most of these space rocks disintegrated high in the atmosphere and caused few problems on the ground. Some events people will have heard about, such as the twenty-meter-wide object that ripped across the sky above the Russian city of Chelyabinsk in 2013 or the forty-meter-wide asteroid that lit up the skies over Buffalo, New York on a winter day in 2024. But many of the asteroid strikes on Earth went unseen and unreported because they occurred over oceans.

The CTBTO has monitored atmospheric asteroid impacts since 2013. What they don't know is another government agency is also monitoring the feed. And that agency does more than listen.

Early Sunday morning, the CTBTO detected an atmospheric asteroid explosion over the South Carolina wetlands.

A remote monitoring station managed by an obscure government agency also detects the explosion. Because the impact is over a populated region, a surveillance satellite outfitted with cameras and infrared imaging scans the impact area to determine if there is any damage.

A young woman sits in a dark room. Her young face glows from the light of several screens arrayed before her as she views the satellite footage in real time. She wears a blue tunic, and she wears her long hair pulled back. She is professional and stoic as she surveys the impact site. Three heat signatures appear on a screen. She presses an icon and reports. "We have three down at north thirty-three degrees, forty-seven minutes, eleven point three nine seconds by West seventy-eight degrees, forty-four minutes, fifty-nine seconds."

There is silence for a moment, then a monotone voice replies, "Confirmed. Dispatching."

Before Daylight–Wetlands near Myrtle Beach, SC

Fog lingers lazily over the silent wetland pond. A team of four men dressed in flat-gray, digitally generated camouflaged suits work efficiently and nearly invisibly in the predawn light.

XVIII

The four men do not work to eradicate the scene. The dead are dead. No one can change that, but they can control the perception of the cause of death. Brody's body is already stiffening. Rigor mortis is setting in. All the easier to stand him up. One-man squats down and struggles to keep Brody standing while another man positions a shotgun in the dead boy's hands, pointing the barrel at his face.

The team's leader, a tall, muscular man with a bald head, receives a call on his VUE lens. He views a stout, Caucasian man wearing a white business shirt and thick, black-framed glasses. The chubby man speaks. "Kobalt, is the site under control?"

The team leader, dressed in the same gray camouflage as his team, wears no markings to indicate rank or military affiliation, yet his physique and the way he moves conveys that he is military or ex-military. He speaks, with a deep raspy tone. "We're almost finished."

The shotgun blasts. A mist composed of pulverized blood, brain and bone fills the air. The kneeling man holding Brody allows the teenage body to jolt backward. Brody's body falls stiffly in the grassy mud. The frogs are silent, watching.

The white man displayed in the VUE lens speaks. "The gun shots will be reported to the police. Local news will report an accidental shooting followed by suicide. A late-night teenage adventure gone wrong. Another episode of an illegal gun used by juveniles."

Kobalt nods. With hand gestures, he directs his men to sweep the ground to cover their footprints. He looks in his VUE lens to continue his report. "Understood, sir. That's what local law enforcement will find when they arrive to investigate the scene."

The white man with the black frame glasses gives an approving nod. "Tragic for the families. What happened is out of our control. We can only control the perception."

Kobalt and his team move through the grass of the wetlands, sweeping the trail of their boot prints while leaving the imprints of the boys' shoes, leading the way for investigators to discover the gory scene.

Kobalt speaks softly but with a force picked up through the microphone of his VUE lens. "We can't keep this up. My team is exhausted. The frequency of the events is increasing. We've been chasing these things around the globe. How long do you think can we keep going like this?"

The man in the VUE replies, "Kobalt, the time is near. We have controlled the news and information to keep the masses peaceful. We have worked ceaselessly to keep them unaware of what's coming, and we have been supremely successful. Even the highest levels of government around the world are oblivious to what's about to happen. It's almost time. Once you have secured the scene, bring your men and join us in the city."

After the sun rose on the wetlands that morning, police investigators and the coroner came to the desired conclusion. There is no news about the threat of asteroids impacting Earth killing teenage boys.

Later that morning, the portly man dressed in the white button-down shirt and black rim glasses watches a video stream from the Myrtle Beach news. He watches a young female reporter recount the story:

A sonic boom woke residents of Myrtle Beach early this morning. There are reports of shattered nerves and broken windows, but no injuries. Authorities attribute the event to supersonic aircraft flying out of nearby Shaw Air Force Base. The Air Force has not responded to inquiries. In other news, local police report that three boys were found dead this morning. Authorities believe the boys were playing with an old, outlawed shotgun they found in the wetlands. Police are calling this a terrible accident. They believe one boy fired a shot, striking his two friends. The boy with the gun then took his own life. It's a sad day for our community. We send our condolences to the boys' families.

The report moves on to an interview with the chief of police, who warns citizens not to pick up or use illegal firearms.

The news is controlled.

Control. This is the objective of the man who observes. He watches the screens displayed in his VUE, satisfied with the outcome of this event.

Thanks for reading